SNAPREVISE

SnapRevise Text Guide:
Hamlet by William Shakespeare

Aleksandra Najdovska

InStudent Education UK Ltd owner of SnapRevise® trademark.
43 Priston Close, Worle, BS22 7FL, Weston-Super-Mare, United Kingdom

www.snaprevise.co.uk

Copyright © InStudent Publishing Pty Ltd 2024

All rights reserved. These notes are protected by copyright owned by InStudent Publishing Pty Ltd and you may not reproduce, disseminate, or communicate to the public the whole or a substantial part thereof except as permitted at law or with the prior written consent of InStudent Publishing Pty Ltd.

Title: Hamlet by William Shakespeare Text Guide
ISBN: 978-1-917424-22-6

Published by InStudent Education UK Ltd CN 15550989 under licence from InStudent Publishing Pty Ltd.
ACN 624 188101

Disclaimer

No reliance on warranty. These SnapRevise materials are intended to supplement but are not intended to replace or to be any substitute for your regular school attendance, for referring to prescribed texts, or for your own note taking. You are responsible for following the appropriate syllabus, attending school classes, and maintaining good study practices. It is your responsibility to evaluate the accuracy of any information, opinions, and advice in these materials. Under no circumstance will InStudent Publishing Pty Ltd or InStudent Education UK Ltd ("Publishers"), their officers, agents, or employees be liable for any loss or damage caused by your use or reliance on these materials, including any adverse impact upon your performance in any academic subject as a result of your use or reliance on the materials. You accept that all information provided or made available by the Publishers is in the nature of general information and does not constitute advice. It is not guaranteed to be error-free and you should always independently verify any information, including through use of a professional teacher and other reliable resources. To the extent permissible at law, the Publishers expressly disclaim all warranties or guarantees of any kind, whether express or implied, including without limitation any warranties concerning the accuracy or content of information provided in these materials or other fitness for purpose. The Publishers shall not be liable for any direct, indirect, special, incidental, consequential or punitive damages of any kind. You agree to indemnify the Publishers, its officers, agents, and employees against any loss whatsoever by using these materials.

Preface

Hey! My name is Aleksandra, and I completed my final year of high school in 2018, graduating with top results in both of my English subjects. Throughout high school, English was one of my greatest strengths, and was always something I was passionate about. I loved researching the texts I studied, as well as investigating the authors' lives. This really helped me to craft high quality essays and develop skills that ultimately allowed me to achieve great results.

Shakespeare's plays can be difficult to decipher at the best of times. His use of Early Modern English can be hard to follow, even though it's not that different to the English that we use today (okay, maybe it is pretty different, but bear with me here). This Text Guide will assist you in your studies as much as possible in this respect, and should invite a deeper understanding of his play, *Hamlet*.

Hamlet in particular is one of Shakespeare's most intriguing and famous tragedies. "To be or not to be" and "to thine own self be true" are among some of the most frequently quoted lines in literature. The play explores corruption, murder, and war, though remains universal in its exploration of human mortality, contemplation, and jealousy. By taking the time to fully immerse yourself within its contextual framework, *Hamlet* evolves into a complex story. This is why it has remained relevant since its first performance in the early 1600s.

Although English is not everyone's favourite subject, I do hope that this Text Guide sparks your interest in *Hamlet* and Shakespeare and encourages you to do further research. After all, English is arguably the most important subject to study (sorry Maths fans)! This way, you can maximise your marks and distinguish yourself as an excellent writer.

Good luck!

— Aleksandra Najdovska

Contents

1. **Nutshell Summary** — 1
2. **Background Information** — 3
   - Shakespeare's life — 3
     - Philosophical ideas — 4
   - Context — 4
     - Political, historical, and economic conditions — 4
     - Sociocultural context of the Elizabethan era — 5
     - Religion — 5
     - Women and their roles in society — 6
     - The arts and theatre — 6
     - Class structure and hierarchy — 7
     - Exploration and science — 7
3. **Scene-by-Scene Analysis** — 8
   - Act 1 Scene 1 — 8
   - Act 1 Scene 2 — 9
   - Act 1 Scene 3 — 11
   - Act 1 Scene 4 — 11
   - Act 1 Scene 5 — 12
   - Act 2 Scene 1 — 13
   - Act 2 Scene 2 — 13
   - Act 3 Scene 1 — 16
   - Act 3 Scene 2 — 17
   - Act 3 Scene 3 — 19
   - Act 3 Scene 4 — 20
   - Act 4 Scene 1 — 21
   - Act 4 Scene 2 — 22
   - Act 4 Scene 3 — 22
   - Act 4 Scene 4 — 23
   - Act 4 Scene 5 — 24
   - Act 4 Scene 6 — 25
   - Act 4 Scene 7 — 26
   - Act 5 Scene 1 — 27
   - Act 5 Scene 2 — 29

4 Character Analysis — 31
- Hamlet — 31
- Claudius — 32
- Gertrude — 32
- Polonius — 32
- Ophelia — 33
- Laertes — 33
- The Ghost — 34
- Horatio — 34
- Fortinbras — 34
- Rosencrantz and Guildenstern — 35
- Minor characters — 35
  - The Players — 35
  - Marcellus and Barnardo — 35
  - Francisco and Reynaldo — 35
  - Gravediggers — 35

5 Key Themes Analysis — 36
- Revenge — 36
- Appearance and reality — 38
- Mortality, humanity, and fate — 40
- Religion — 41
- Women and sex — 41
- Surveillance and trust — 42
- Action and inaction — 43

6 Structural Features Analysis — 45
- Acts and scenes — 45
- Staging and stage directions — 46
- Character foils — 46
- Hamlet's soliloquies — 46
  - Soliloquies and their function — 46
  - Act 1 Scene 2 — 47
  - Act 1 Scene 5 — 47
  - Act 2 Scene 2 — 48
  - Act 3 Scene 1 — 48
  - Act 3 Scene 2 — 49
  - Act 3 Scene 3 — 49
  - Act 4 Scene 4 — 49
- Metatheatre — 50
- Intertextuality — 50
- Language and literary devices — 51
  - Language — 51
  - Irony and humour — 51
  - Repetition — 52
  - Symbolism — 52
  - Imagery — 53

7	**Quote Bank**	**54**
	Revenge, action, and inaction	54
	Appearance and reality	55
	Mortality, humanity, and fate	56
	Religion	57
	Women and sex	57
	Surveillance and trust	58
	Imagery	58
8	**Sample Essays**	**59**
	Essay One	59
	Essay Two	65
	Essay Three	70
	Essay Four	75
	General essay writing tips	80

ction 1

Nutshell Summary

For a great summary of Hamlet, you need look no further than the closing remarks of the character, Horatio.

> *"So shall you hear*
> *Of carnal, bloody, and unnatural acts,*
> *Of accidental judgments, casual slaughters,*
> *Of deaths put on by cunning and forced cause,*
> *And, in this upshot, purposes mistook*
> *Fall'n on th' inventors' heads."*

The whole plot is filled with acts of violence, murder, vengeance, guilt, and deceit. It takes place against the backdrop of war between the armies of Denmark and Norway, during the late Middle Ages (14th and 15th centuries). It is primarily set within and around the castle of Elsinore, Denmark. King Hamlet and his Queen Gertrude formerly ruled the court. However, a serpent allegedly stung the King whilst he was napping in an orchard, and he unfortunately died. As a result, his brother Claudius married Queen Gertrude (his former sister in law – yikes!) and becomes the new King of Denmark.

Something fascinating to note is that *Hamlet* was originally published in three editions:

- Q1, or 'The First Quarto' (1603)
- Q2, or 'The Second Quarto' (1604)
- F1, or 'The First Folio' (1623)

Most modern versions of the play are a **conflation** of Q2 and F1. Initially, Q1 was originally thought to be a faulty version copied from the memory of one of the actors. However, modern scholars believe that it's not necessarily the inferior version, but more like a 'performing' version of the play, as it has a much more dramatic plot.

Conflation: the merging multiple sets of ideas or texts into the one entity.

Initially, the guards of the castle and Horatio encourage Hamlet to wait until midnight to witness the reappearing ghost dressed in King Hamlet's armour. Hamlet complies and meets the vengeful apparition of his father's ghost who divulges the real details of his death; Claudius poisoned him in an orchard so that he could marry Gertrude via an incestuous act, and ultimately become King of Denmark. The dead king then urges Hamlet to take revenge for his murder by killing Claudius and becoming the rightful King.

In order to achieve this, Hamlet pretends to be insane throughout the play. His thoughts are filled with contemplation about the meaning of life and of the nature of existence.

Though this madness is depicted as a tactic in Hamlet's revenge plot, the other characters begin to theorise other possible reasons. Polonius, Claudius' right-hand-man, believes that it is Hamlet's love and obsession for his daughter, Ophelia that has caused his madness. Polonius tells Ophelia to avoid Hamlet to save herself some heartache, because according to Polonius, Hamlet would ultimately reject a lower-class woman like her. Meanwhile, Polonius' son, Laertes travels to France, where he is studying with an expert swordsman.

Allegory: a story that can be reinterpreted to uncover a hidden political or moral meaning.

As part of Hamlet's grand plan to expose Claudius, he initiates a scheme when a group of actors arrived at the castle. He provides the "players" with a monologue that imitated the murder of his father in the hopes that it would make Claudius feel guilty and ultimately confess, acting as an **allegory** for the play itself. Claudius gets progressively more uncomfortable during the play, revealing he is guilty of committing **fratricide** through a **soliloquy**.

Fratricide: killing one's own brother.

Soliloquy: when a character in a play speaks their thoughts aloud for the audience to hear.

When Gertrude confronts Hamlet about his plans, they engage in a heated argument about her unfaithful and incestuous behaviour with Claudius. However, Polonius spies on them from behind a tapestry in order to discover the real reasons for Hamlet's insanity so that he can report back to Claudius. It is at this point in the play that the audience really begins to question Hamlet's mental state. He insists that the ghost of his father is in the room and divulges to Gertrude the details of his revenge plot. However, Gertrude cannot actually see the ghost. At this point, audiences are made to believe that Hamlet is pretending to be insane, though his true madness comes to fruition in this scene. At the climax, Hamlet stabs Polonius from behind the tapestry, thinking that it was Claudius. As a consequence of Polonius' death, his daughter Ophelia falls deeper into her own madness. Meanwhile, Claudius sends Hamlet away to England for some 'rest and recovery,' but has a secret plan to have him killed while he is there. He finds out, and instead forges a letter so that Guildenstern and Rosencrantz are murdered instead. Ophelia's sadness deepens, and she ultimately drowns in a possible suicide attempt. As two gravediggers are digging her plot, Hamlet and Horatio find them, though Hamlet is unaware of Ophelia's death. He further contemplates his life, when he finds Yorick's skull – a very popular symbol in Hamlet. The old jester of the court led to Hamlet's ultimate examination of his own existence, and awareness of his own **mortality**.

Mortality: a being that is subject to inevitable death (i.e. 'mortal' and unable to live forever).

In the last act, a fencing duel takes place between Hamlet and Laertes, who had come home from France to avenge his now dead father and sister. He and Claudius plot to poison Hamlet via a cut from with the tip of Laertes' blade. A goblet is also filled with poison in another attempt to murder Hamlet. However, during the fencing match, Gertrude drinks from the poisoned goblet and dies instantly. The poisoned blade scars both Hamlet and Laertes, while Claudius is stabbed by Hamlet, leading to their simultaneous deaths as well. Once nearly everyone has been killed, the story concludes with Fortinbras arriving from Poland to take his share of the land for Norway.

Section 2
Background Information

When studying any of Shakespeare's texts, it is important to be fully immersed within the times during which he lived and the lifestyle that he led. This foundational knowledge will actually help you understand some significant references made in his plays. While it is beneficial to include context within your essays to enrich your arguments and demonstrate a broad understanding of the text, make sure you are not writing entire paragraphs about background information. Otherwise, you are wasting valuable words when you should be strengthening your essay with analysis!

Shakespeare's life

William Shakespeare was born in April 1564 to successful glove-maker John Shakespeare and the daughter of a prosperous landowning farmer, Mary Arden, in Stratford-upon-Avon, England. His date of birth is not formally known, though he was baptised on April 26th. It is believed that he was educated at the King's New School, a newly established grammar school in Stratford, though did not attend university further than this. At 18 years old, Shakespeare married Anne Hathaway, who was eight years his senior. Together they had three children: Susanna in 1583, and twins Hamnet and Judith in 1585. Unfortunately, Hamnet died of unknown causes at the age of 11.

Around 1590, Shakespeare left his family in Stratford-upon-Avon in the pursuit of becoming a playwright and actor in London. However, between 1585 and 1592, there are very few historical traces of Shakespeare's life, and as such these years are referred to as his "lost years." In 1592, he was mentioned as a significant contributor to theatre in London, with several of his plays already being performed on stage. After 1594, a company of actors, or players, called Lord Chamberlain's Men, were the only ones to perform Shakespeare's plays. However, this group was renamed **the King's Men** following the death of Queen Elizabeth I, because the new King James I offered a royal patent to the company. Shakespeare was favoured by both monarchs, which further allowed him to prosper as a playwright. Shakespeare's wealth was also demonstrated through his part ownership of the Globe Theatre, which was established in 1599 upon the bank of the River Thames by a handful of members from within the company.

Shakespeare retired back to Stratford-upon-Avon in 1613, and died only three years later at the age of 52. Throughout his life, he wrote approximately 37 plays and 154 sonnets. He is regarded as the greatest writer in the English language and one of the world's best dramatists. His body of work has left an immense legacy and has transcended the times during which he wrote, and many of his texts are seminal foundations for Western literature and culture.

Philosophical ideas

The period of time during which Shakespeare lived was rich with philosophy, which greatly influenced his plays. This is very clear in *Hamlet*, which was particularly influenced by the English Renaissance movement.

The original Renaissance era originated in fifteenth century Italy, wherein the revival of ancient Greek and Latin texts from the Middle Ages provoked a massive cultural change. Many scholars found new motivation from an idea called *humanitas*, that proposed all of the **idiosyncrasies** unique to human beings should be studied further. This led to the movement's new name, **Renaissance Humanism,** which generated a new **interest in, and optimism towards, the human experience.** For these humanists, finding greater reason for human existence would ultimately benefit society as a whole.

> **Idiosyncrasy:** behaviour that is unique to an individual.

Once this Renaissance Humanism movement expanded around Europe in the sixteenth and seventeenth centuries, a new form of sceptical humanism emerged. This idea instead focused on the limitations of human understanding, as opposed to the previous optimism. It was thought that the human experience was merely comprised of different façades because mankind could not cope with the difficult truths of reality. Keep these ideas in mind while reading *Hamlet*, because it will really help you to understand Hamlet's **motivations,** and create strong links in your analysis of the play.

Furthermore, *Hamlet* is still being analysed through different lenses and philosophical ideas today. Literary theories including psychoanalysis, existentialism, feminism, and structuralism, among others, all allow for unique interpretations of the play. This enduring appeal is a big reason as to why Shakespeare's works have remained relevant; they possess a great deal of **textual integrity.**

> **Textual integrity:** the unity and value of a text, and how its form and language contribute to long-lasting meaning.

Context

Political, historical, and economic conditions

Within Shakespeare's lifetime, there was a lot of change and uncertainty within England and Europe more broadly. In many ways, *Hamlet* is a direct reflection of the shifts occurring in society at the time. When the play was first performed, Queen Elizabeth I's reign was coming to an end. However, with her death came the end of her lineage, and by extension the Tudor royal line, since she had no children. Her death led to major political upheaval, with many people fearing a religious war between Catholicism and Protestantism. These events are directly mirrored in the play, as Hamlet's murder in the final scene symbolises the end of his lineage in Denmark.

Since the play is set in the mid 1500's, it takes place after the **Protestant Reformation** of 1517. The Reformation aimed to restructure the practices and beliefs of the Roman Catholic Church, as it was believed that their priorities had moved away from religion, and that they instead wished to extend their power across Europe. The implications of these religions are seen throughout *Hamlet*, with Shakespeare subtly referencing the King and the Prince's differing religions, ultimately leading to internal conflict for Hamlet.

Sociocultural context of the Elizabethan era

The Elizabethan era spans the duration of **Queen Elizabeth I's reign, 1558 to 1603.** Famous for its theatre because of the works of Shakespeare, this era also saw the **blossoming of art, music, and literature**. During her reign, there was a brief peace during the Reformation, which is why her death brought so much concern. However, there were economic struggles at the time; with the rising population came food shortages and a **perpetual** cycle of poverty. While there were varied jobs available in the physical labour and entertainment industries, many people still found themselves without sufficient incomes. However, the Queen also encouraged an articulate and educated aristocracy. As such, many individuals who were fortunate enough to receive an education studied Latin language and literature. Shakespeare's knowledge of classical theatre, poetry, and legend was developed because of this, and is greatly evident through his work.

Perpetual: ongoing or never-ending.

To a lesser extent, the emerging Jacobean Era from 1603 also influenced Shakespeare. This was characterised by the reign of James VI of Scotland, who inherited the English throne as James I. This unification of both kingdoms was a somewhat practical move to create peace, which was desperately needed following the change and uncertainty of the final years of the Elizabethan era.

Religion

As aforementioned, religion was a significant **facet** of Elizabethan society. Much of Elizabethan culture was dictated by people's beliefs in **Christianity.** Many religious symbols and allusions can be seen throughout the play, including the idea of the **Great Chain of Being,** which is a hierarchy of living beings (with God and monarchs at the top, and peasants at the bottom). This was based on the principle that the natural order of things must be maintained. Any disruption to this order may have resulted in disastrous consequences, as reflected this in the chaos of the *Hamlet* plot, due to the murder of the King.

Facet: a component or aspect of a larger whole.

Women and their roles in society

The role of women in Elizabethan society was simple: **to serve and obey men**, since men were considered the 'superior sex.' Women were said to have naturally softer dispositions, be more compassionate, and were supposed to be submissive to their husbands as part of their religion. Contrastingly, men were considered to be more fierce, passionate, straightforward, and headstrong.

Aligned with their gender stereotypes, men and women had very different roles in Elizabethan England. In regards to education, noble girls were tutored at home in languages and arts but could not pursue education any further. Acting of any sort was dishonourable, so men played the roles of women in Shakespeare's plays instead. Unfortunately, commoners did not receive an education, and were instead taught the domestic duties expected of them once they were married, including all the skills necessary to run a household. Additionally, women were forbidden from voting, owning an estate, or owning a business, amongst other restrictions.

Once women were married, they were expected to provide some money and assets to bring to the marriage, which was called a dowry. Early marriages were very common, and were often done in order to improve status. Women were then expected to raise their children, while their husbands would join the labour force in order to provide for the family. While they were expected to uphold or improve the family's social status and be the 'head of the household,' men still had a duty to care for their wives and children.

The arts and theatre

The arts flourished during Queen Elizabeth I's reign, which helped to build an enriched culture in England. The Renaissance brought a development of the understanding of literature in society. Previously, visual depictions of the Bible were popular for an illiterate, religious society. However, with the discovery of valuable ancient Greek and Latin texts, more **secular** topics were addressed. Literature as a whole was more valued, due to a rise in education and the Protestant belief in the importance of reading and interpreting the Bible for oneself. The printing press also allowed for more widespread access to written media.

Secular: not connected with, or bound to, religion or spirituality.

The theatre industry especially thrived in the Elizabethan era as an entertaining art from. It proved to be a booming business opportunity as well as a favoured leisure activity.

The chaos contrived by Shakespeare is modelled after the works of the ancient Roman politician and philosopher, Seneca. The themes highlighted by Horatio, as well as the bloodthirsty **regicide** and appearance of a ghost throughout the play, are very reminiscent of the themes covered in Seneca's plays. As such, *Hamlet* can be classified as a 'Senecan revenge tragedy.'

Class structure and hierarchy

Elizabethan England had a very strict social hierarchy. Where people lived, who people married, and even what people wore contributed to their social status. A series of laws called 'Statutes of Apparel' dictated the clothes that different people should wear. For example, those in the higher class were to wear bright colours made of silk, satin, and velvet. Comparatively, commoners' clothes were made of leather, wool, or cotton, and as such had duller colours like brown and beige.

In terms of the social hierarchy, there were several distinct classes to which people were expected to adhere. Above all was the **monarch** – in this case, Queen Elizabeth I who was God's representative on earth. After her was the **nobility,** who were families that owned large amounts of land and thus were powerful within society. The **gentry** were the following class, which was the group of aristocrats – knights, squires, gentlemen and gentlewomen. They were also quite wealthy. The middleclass, or **Yeomanry,** made up the majority of the population, with most families being able to get by somewhat comfortably. Finally, there were the **labourers** and **beggars** – people who engaged in physical labour and often lived in poverty. Shakespeare distinctly explores class structure and hierarchy in *Hamlet*, using different language techniques to distinguish individuals.

Exploration and science

Continuing with the theme of great change, Elizabethan England was also characterised by significant intellectual advancements. New technology of the time allowed for greater exploration of foreign countries, which sparked a renewed interest in the world. This is the reason why Shakespeare picked many 'exotic' locations, including Denmark for Hamlet; it was even more entertaining for the audience to imagine a distant land.

In comparison, the medical profession during Queen Elizabeth I's reign was far from accurate scientific methodology. Supernatural causes of events were still considered legitimate reasoning. They believed that different organs had different effects on people's 'souls,' and the composition of different fluids within the body – blood, yellow bile, black bile, and phlegm – were said to determine the personality of the individuals by affecting their brains and altering people's dispositions.

Section 3

Scene-by-Scene Analysis

The following section is a scene-by-scene analysis of *Hamlet*. It features a more in-depth description of what happens in the actual plot. It is important to understand the full breadth of the narrative in order to grasp the characters' motivations and the significance of different events. I've also included some contextual links for an even better conceptual understanding of the text and its significance to an Elizabethan audience.

In your essays, while it is important to keep the marker up to speed with the scenes that you are referencing, you have to be careful not to merely retell the story. Remember, **essays are for analysis,** not for a retelling of the entire play. By looking at the sample essays at the back of this guide, you should get a better idea of how to integrate your analysis into your essays as much as possible.

Act 1 Scene 1

The first scene of this play begins on a dark night outside the castle of Elsinore, Denmark. The setting is actually modelled after the Kronborg Castle in Denmark. Barnardo, an officer of the castle, is relieving Francisco from his guard for the night. It is very dark at this time, and Francisco must ask "who's there?" to be sure of what's going on. Though this is a simple line, it immediately conveys the confusion that is present for the entirety of the play. The **sickness and corruption of Denmark** is also established early on by Francisco, who remarks "'Tis bitter cold, and I am sick at heart." The guards wait until Horatio and Marcellus enter, at which point they begin to share a supernatural story. As usual with Shakespearean plays, we get to hear about some questionable events before we get to see them, which furthers the air of confusion and deceit. "Sit down awhile/ And let us once again assail your ears" is what Horatio is told to do, as the guards speak; they believe that for two evenings past, the ghost of the dead King Hamlet has arrived at the castle in his signature armour. The King was allegedly bitten by a serpent while sleeping in an orchard, which led to his death. Horatio does not believe that the ghost has been appearing; however, it arrives once again, stalking like a warrior, and shocks all the men on guard. They try to talk to him, but he does not respond and vanishes for a while.

Horatio, now trembling and looking pale, believes "this bodes some strange eruption to our state," which ultimately foreshadows the tragedy that is about to take place in Denmark. He then begins to share some rumours surrounding an imminent war. King Fortinbras from Norway and old King Hamlet battled thirty years ago, during which they both declared to give up their land to their conqueror. As such, once Old Hamlet killed Old Fortinbras, he was able to take ownership of some land in Norway.

The problem now is Old Fortinbras' son (whose name is also Fortinbras – how creative!). Like father, like son, in more than just name, Fortinbras, along with some thugs from the country, want to take back some of the land that his father lost all those years ago. This introduces yet another prominent theme in the play: **revenge.** Suddenly, the ghost briefly reappears. However, a crow calls as an omen of dawn, a dangerous time for ghosts, and sends the ghost away for the third night. They plan to tell young Hamlet about the night's events once he has woken up.

As you can tell, there's already a lot going on in the first scene of *Hamlet*. This is because the play actually begins **in medias res.** In this case, Hamlet's father has already died and is causing chaos within the state of Denmark. By having him appear as a ghost, Shakespeare implies that the King has 'unfinished business.' He was not able to pray before his death and be forgiven for his sins, as per his Catholic beliefs, and as such has not passed on to the afterlife successfully. Instead, he is living in purgatory, and his death has upset the balance of nature, disrupting the Great Chain of Being.

In medias res: Latin for 'in the middle of things,' this is a literary technique to describe a story that starts in the middle, rather than with a conventional introduction of 'who, what, when, where, and why.'

Another significant contextual concern that is reflected in *Hamlet* is the anxiety surrounding the monarchy of Queen Elizabeth I. With her looming death, many Englishmen and women were worried that any shift in power would disrupt the peace. This is directly represented by Shakespeare's' contrived chaos in the aftermath of the death of King Hamlet.

Act 1 Scene 2

This scene begins inside the castle, where Claudius, King Hamlet's brother, is jovially announcing his marriage to Gertrude, his former sister-in-law. This largely contrasts the dark, supernatural tone of Scene 1. Claudius' main concern is to balance the mourning of his brother with the happiness of his new matrimony, though this newly convoluted family dynamic does not sit well with Hamlet. Nevertheless, Claudius gets on with business. He addresses the issue of young Fortinbras wanting to take some land away from Denmark. He is doing so in rebellion of his bed-ridden uncle, who took the throne after Old Fortinbras was killed. As such, King Claudius wishes to make an agreement with Fortinbras' uncle, which would help to stop the young man's military plans. He sends Voltemand and Cornelius with a letter to Norway. Claudius' speeches are filled with unsettling **contradictions** and **oxymorons.** For example, "Though yet of Hamlet our late brother's death / The memory be green," combines both **death imagery** and **words of growth and renewal.** Similarly, the contradictions of "mirth in funeral" and "dirge in marriage" is just enough for the audience to feel uneasy around Claudius. After all, if it weren't for Claudius' marriage to Gertrude, it would be Hamlet sitting on the Danish throne. His efforts to present a happy court seem somewhat superficial, because his attempt at "balancing" the emotions actually does not align with the Great Chain of Being. This symbolises the corruption lurking in Denmark.

Oxymorons: a figure of speech where two contradictory terms are used in conjunction. For example, cruel kindness.

Aside: a remark that is intended to be heard by the audience but not by oxther characters. Usually, asides are only one or two lines.

After this, Laertes, the son of the Lord Chamberlain Polonius, wishes to go back to France in order to further pursue his swordsmanship studies. He had arrived in Denmark to witness the marriage, but Claudius and Polonius gladly gives him leave when he asks, because he had already fulfilled his duty to the King. King Claudius then turns to Hamlet to answer his question, addressing him as "my cousin Hamlet, and my son." Shakespeare gives Hamlet an **aside** as his first words of the play and he says, "A little more than kin and less than kind." This line sets up **Hamlet's perspective of his relationship with Claudius;** he is "more than kin," as he is now not only his uncle, but his stepfather, much to Hamlet's distaste; he is not going to stoop to Claudius' poor attempt of a healthy court. The word "kind" in this line has a triple meaning. It could refer to the fact that he is **not a direct blood relative,** (i.e. they are not of the same "ancestral stock"). It could also refer to the definition of kind as 'natural,' whereby Hamlet is insinuating that **Claudius' lustful marriage to Gertrude is in fact, unnatural.** Otherwise, it could be using the modern definition of kindness, which implies that **Hamlet has a low opinion of Claudius' personality and compassion.**

Filial obligation: specific duties that children must uphold simply because they are the offspring of their parents. 'Filial' relates to being a son or daughter.

Claudius addresses the "clouds" that are still surrounding Hamlet, because he is still heavily mourning the death of his father. However, Hamlet jokes with Claudius using slightly black humour, and states, "Not so, my lord. I am too much i' the sun" (as a pun on son/sun). When Gertrude addresses Hamlet about his dark clothes, he answers slightly more sincerely. Gertrude says, "all that lives must die," and in doing so addresses the prominent theme of mortality. Gertrude is confused as to why he is still mourning, wearing black clothes, and sulking while everyone else in the castle is celebrating the new marriage. Claudius also interjects; he thinks that while Hamlet does have a **filial obligation** to mourn his father, to do so excessively is stubborn, not manly, and against God's will. He says, "We pray you, throw to earth / This unprevailing woe," and to think of Claudius "as of a father." Once again, Hamlet does not agree to this invitation from Claudius. However, Gertrude implores Hamlet to listen, and strongly encourages Hamlet to stay at the castle instead of going back to Wittenberg University as he had planned. He listens to Gertrude and only addresses her when accepting his duty, because he does not respect Claudius' input and believes that Claudius is far inferior to his dead father.

Following this, Hamlet performs his first **soliloquy.** He announces his wish to die, but warns himself against it due to his moral compass and his faith in God, and thus contextualises the Christian framework that the play exists within. At this moment for Hamlet, **life is pointless.** The fact that his father has only been dead for less than two months, and his mother has already remarried an inferior suitor in an act of incest, disgusts him. He is disappointed in his mother's weaknesses in this situation and believes that it can only lead to bad things. This soliloquy will be explored in depth on page 47.

Hamlet sees Horatio, Marcellus, and Bernardo approaching, and ceases the soliloquy. Hamlet questions why his schoolmate is in the castle, and Horatio answers that he was there for King Hamlet's funeral. However, Hamlet is keenly aware that he was mostly there for the new royal marriage. Then, Horatio informs Hamlet of the ghost from the previous night, and urges Hamlet to stand watch tonight, which he agrees to do. He trusts the words of his friend, who also **acts as the voice of reason throughout the play.**

Act 1 Scene 3

Laertes is ready to depart for France at the beginning of this scene. As he is saying goodbye to his sister, Ophelia, he warns her not to fall in love with Hamlet, who could never truly love her due to their differences in status. As aforementioned, societal status was a very prominent feature in Elizabethan relationships, and Hamlet was born too high up the hierarchy to love Ophelia. There is a significant amount of sexual imagery in Laertes' dialogue, as he refers to her "chaste treasure open" to Hamlet's "unmaster'd importunity." This reflects the incestuous undertones of Claudius and Gertrude's marriage. Ophelia wishes that Laertes would be careful with his own heart whilst away in France. In this sense, **Laertes acts as a foil for Hamlet,** (see page 46) as he is affectionate and takes action without much thought.

Polonius, Laertes' father, then enters to bid his son farewell. He chastises Laertes for taking too long to leave, but then gives him more blessings, and orders him to act with integrity whilst away on leave. He warns Laertes to remain virtuous, and to not share all of his thoughts with any individual. He does not want his son to show off, but wants him to remain true to himself. Polonius' tone is courteous towards his son, for the most part. It is in this monologue that Polonius says, "To thine own self be true" – a now famous line in English literature. It implies that Laertes should be honest in his relationships, should always do the right thing, but that he should think of his own benefit first. However, the advice that he provides masks its real purpose. They are actually more like long-winded orders for his son to follow dutifully. This scene highlights the paternal instincts of Polonius, in contrast to the lack of paternal influence upon Hamlet's life now that King Hamlet is dead.

As Laertes leaves, Polonius turns to Ophelia to talk. He adopts a position of authority over his daughter, and employs a very different imperative tone with her. This aligns with the notion in Elizabethan England that women were to be submissive to men. He dismisses her feelings towards Hamlet, and Ophelia does nothing but obey her father because it is what she feels she has to do.

Act 1 Scene 4

This transitional scene is pivotal, as it starts to entwine the dark, supernatural atmosphere of the castle exteriors with the corrupt and artificially happy court interiors. Now that it's nearing midnight, Hamlet is standing watch with Horatio and Marcellus and is eagerly awaiting the appearance of the ghost. Claudius is busy celebrating Hamlet's decision to stay in Denmark, drinking into the night in an old tradition called 'the king's rouse.' The intoxicated behaviours of those in the court emphasises the imagery of an ill Denmark plagued by vice. Horatio laments how this kind of behaviour lessens the significance of people's noble achievements.

It is just past midnight when the ghost enters for the fourth night in a row. This time, Hamlet is there to witness it. At first, Hamlet is not sure whether it is a good or bad spirit. He wants to know what has driven his father's spirit out of the grave and to the outskirts of the castle. Hamlet will only get answers from the ghost in private, so Hamlet complies and follows the ghost away, even though his friends strongly advise him against doing so. As Hamlet goes to talk to the ghost, Marcellus insinuates "something is rotten in the state of Denmark." He continues the motif of **disease imagery** and is keenly aware of the problems that are about to ensue.

Act 1 Scene 5

The ghost begins to speak to Hamlet, telling him about the "sulfurous and tormenting flames" of purgatory that he has had to endure since his untimely death. He warns Hamlet that he has to be ready to take revenge, informing him that he did not actually die from a serpent sting, but rather was murdered by Claudius in a "foul, strange and unnatural" manner. Hamlet is shocked, but not surprised about this revelation. The Ghost continues, and demonstrates increasing anger towards Claudius for seducing Gertrude. However, with dawn about to come, the ghost rapidly details the murder: Claudius had crept up on him whilst in the orchard and poured a "leprous distilment" of henbane poison into his ear, which made his blood coil and his skin crust.

Juxtaposes: two contrasting ideas being placed together for comparison.

Unfortunately for Old Hamlet, his life, crown, and wife had all been taken away from him whilst he was living in sin. He had no chance to pray for forgiveness before his death, which is why he was sent to purgatory. Old Hamlet finally urges Hamlet to take action, but to leave Gertrude alone so that she can wallow in her own guilt and instead by judged by God. He then disappears before morning comes. Shakespeare **juxtaposes** this father-son chat with the conversation between Laertes and Polonius, such that instead of jovial blessings and advice, this talk actually unravels a budding revenge plot as delivered by Hamlet's dead father. It highlights the **absence of stability in Hamlet's life** at this point, which is why he was so heavily grieving and questioning the moral actions of those around him. It's a pivotal point of Act 1, and precludes Hamlet's descent into madness.

Antic: bizarre, or out-of-character.

Hamlet makes a promise to himself and to his father to remember the order, before returning to Horatio and Marcellus. He reveals the conversation was incredible, but refuses to relay the specifics to them. Horatio is already picking up that there is something off about Hamlet's personality when he returns, but is still trusted by Hamlet to not tell anyone about seeing the ghost. They swear on Hamlet's sword with the ghost's encouragement. Hamlet admits that he may put on an "**antic** disposition" in the near future, but they are not to tell anyone why. Hamlet says one last goodbye to the ghost, and all the men go their separate ways.

Act 2 Scene 1

Act 2 begins with Polonius sending his servant, Reynaldo, on a mission to France. He gives him some letters and some money to deliver to Laertes. However, he wants him to spy on Laertes for a while before he meets with him. He insists that Reynaldo should ask people around Paris to find out about Laertes' behaviour indirectly so that he can build up a level of trust and get more truth out of people, rather than directly telling them his intentions. Polonius also encourages Reynaldo to spread some small white lies; not enough to tarnish Laertes' reputation, but enough to highlight some small faults within Laertes' character and encourage people to agree with him. This scene is very interesting in terms of Polonius' character development. It is unclear at this stage whether he is an overprotective fool of a father, or actually a master manipulator who is deceitful enough to spy on his own son. As well as this, **Polonius highlights how easy it is to slightly bend or manipulate the truth and sow seeds of doubt and confusion.**

The second section of this scene involves a conversation between Polonius and Ophelia, his daughter. She is visibly upset because Hamlet came into her sewing room unkempt, grabbed her by the wrist, and stared at her for a long time but did not say anything. Both her and Polonius believe that he has gone crazy with love for Ophelia, especially because she has been ignoring him as per her father's prior orders. This highlights Ophelia's obedient and docile nature. Polonius admits that he did not observe Hamlet closely enough, and instead jumped to the conclusion that he was just toying with Ophelia to ruin her reputation. Polonius blames Hamlet's "violent" lovesick "ecstasy" as the cause of his new erratic and crazy behaviour – this is the first overt reference to Hamlet's madness. However, this is quite a simple-minded theory in comparison to the real reason that he is acting out (as part of his revenge plot).

Act 2 Scene 2

This is a really long and important scene in *Hamlet*, which establishes several developments in various plot points. Straight out of the gate, we are introduced to Rosencrantz and Guildenstern, who are two of Hamlet's schoolmates from Wittenberg University. Claudius informs them of the "change" that has occurred to Hamlet's personality, that they chalk up to his father's death and his mother's hasty remarriage. While Claudius is determined to put an end to Hamlet's grief, he commissions the two men, who have known Hamlet since childhood, to find out some information about what's bothering him and then report back to the King. This is somewhat a betrayal on Rosencrantz and Guildenstern's behalf – while they do have to obey the orders of the King and Queen, they are ultimately giving Hamlet more reason to be suspicious and mistrustful (even though the two men were actually manipulated by the royals to oblige).

After this, Claudius' ambassadors arrive back from Norway and explain the new deal made with Fortinbras. Polonius relays the message: the King of Norway was very disappointed when he heard that Fortinbras was attempting to take Danish land forcefully. So, the King forced Fortinbras to promise not to attack Denmark. And Fortinbras swore to never attack Denmark... which impressed the Norwegian King so much that he let him attack Poland instead! The proposed deal is that Fortinbras would be allowed a free pass through

Denmark on the way to Poland. Something important to consider here is **the difference in personalities between Hamlet and Fortinbras**. While Hamlet has been asked to take revenge on behalf of his father, he has not been able to follow through yet because of his **contemplative nature.** In contrast, Fortinbras is **impulsive** and has wanted to take immediate action to avenge his dead father. Nevertheless, Claudius quickly accepts the offer, hinting at his lack of interest in matters of the state. This is very unlike his brother Old Hamlet, who was often successful in war. Instead, Claudius is much more interested in matters of the court; **he is more of a politician.** Additionally, it seems that he cares more about Hamlet's fragile state of mind than the fact that he is practically inviting a volatile army into his country. This is because Claudius is aware that Hamlet currently poses the biggest threat to Claudius' throne.

The next section of this long scene involves a discussion between Polonius, Claudius, and Gertrude regarding Hamlet and Ophelia's relationship. There is increasing concern about Hamlet's sanity, or lack thereof. Polonius begins with some convoluted dialogue, and shares his belief that Hamlet's madness is a result of Ophelia's rejection. He blames himself for ordering her to ignore him, and somewhat convinces Claudius and Gertrude that this is the problem. However, he thinks that he made the orders fairly, as he implies that Ophelia is his own property and that she was being a dutiful daughter by listening to his order. To try and figure this out, Polonius and Claudius decide to spy on Hamlet during his next conversation with Ophelia.

At this point, Hamlet enters the scene while reading a book and engages in a conversation with Polonius. If Hamlet is feigning his madness, he's doing a good job of it. He convincingly behaves and speaks like he has lost his mind. He keeps his answers short and bitter, and begins to repeat his words over and over again. For example, "words, words, words" and "except my life, except my life, except my life." He begins speaking in **double entendres**, with many of his phrases open to more than one interpretation from the audience. Even at the best of times, Hamlet's state of mind was fragile, so it's unclear at this point if Hamlet is still pretending, or if he has actually started to go insane. He also begins speaking in prose, rather than in verse, which further emphasises his spiralling mental health. This is a technique used by Shakespeare often, and will be discussed later as a structural feature.

Polonius then takes his leave, at which point Rosencrantz and Guildenstern enter the stage. They joke with each other and make small talk for a while. At one point, Hamlet comments, "Then is doomsday near," which signifies his concern for the state of Denmark using a biblical allusion. They soon begin to chat about the nature of man, all the while trying to understand Hamlet's new eccentricities. Within this conversation, Hamlet admits to his change in character. He admires the glory of mankind – "how noble in reason, how infinite in faculty" – and the "beauty of the world," reflective of the **Renaissance Humanism** that greatly influenced Shakespeare's writing.

It is an intertextual reference from a major text of an Italian Humanist, Pico della Mirandola, called *Oration on the Dignity of Man*. However, ultimately Hamlet says, "And yet, to me, what is this quintessence of dust? Man delights not me" – in other words, **humans are nothing but dust to him**. This motif of mortality is again addressed in this scene, and is a quintessential part of Hamlet's psyche. **He is constantly questioning his own reasons to live and questioning human existence as a whole.**

The existential conversation dies off when the players arrive to the castle from the city. After some more conversation, Hamlet admits that he is only crazy sometimes, or "but mad north-north-west. When the wind is southerly, I know a hawk from a handsaw." This implies that he is acting, and has not gone completely mad (yet).

Polonius enters for a short time before the actors, whom Hamlet welcomes warmly. He requests that the first player recites a particular scene from an epic Roman poem called *The Aeneid*. It follows the story of Pyrrhus, during the Trojan War, and the speech depicts the moment at which Pyrrhus exacts revenge for his slaughtered father, by murdering King Priam of Troy and his wife, Hecuba. Throughout the speech, there are several references to the Queen's adultery, the murder of a King and father, as well as hesitation. All of these events are **parallels** to those that occur in *Hamlet*, exacerbated when Hamlet commissions the First Player to perform an extra speech in the form of a **sonnet** the following night. Hamlet is already amazed at the actor's capacity to demonstrate emotion within the fictitious story.

Sonnet: a poem of fourteen lines, typically with ten syllables per line.

Hamlet is finally left alone to perform his second soliloquy of the play. The general gist of it is that **he is frustrated with himself because of his inaction.** He admires the actor for his emotional depth and relationship to men that mean nothing to him (i.e. the characters that he plays). Hamlet has far more emotional motives for seeking real revenge, yet can't follow through with his plans. To solve this, Hamlet sets a trap for Claudius to "have these players / Play something like the murder of my father." The idea is that Claudius would be so shaken by watching a re-enactment of the same kind of crime he committed, look guilty, and expose himself. In this way, Hamlet somewhat justifies his delay, because he is just trying to make sure that he is doing the right thing.

This inaction is a very prominent theme for the remainder of the play. However, Hamlet does believe that he will "catch the conscience of the king." Once again, notice that Hamlet has moved back to speaking in verse when he is alone, which indicates that his madness at this point is still an act.

Act 3 Scene 1

This act begins with a conversation between Claudius, Guildenstern, Rosencrantz, Polonius, and Gertrude. The two young men inform the King and Queen that Hamlet has admitted to going mad as of late, but they could not work out why. They also let them know that Hamlet is keen to be entertained by the actors who have come to the castle recently. Rosencrantz and Guildenstern leave after providing the information. Claudius gives Gertrude leave from Claudius and Polonius' conversation about their secret plan to spy on Hamlet and Ophelia. Ophelia is once again used as a pawn in the plans of her conniving male superiors. They use her as bait to get Hamlet to talk and open up about his madness, in the hopes that he will confess his lovesick downfall. At this point, Polonius makes an astute observation using a religious allusion, that "'Tis too much proved, that with devotion's visage / And pious action we do sugar o'er / The devil himself." This means that many people have acted as though they were devoted to religion and God, if only to conceal their negative truths. It is an ironic comment on the state of Elizabethan society and their devotion to religion.

Hamlet then enters and performs his third soliloquy of the play. This one contains possibly the most iconic line of the English language, "**To be or not to be: that is the question.**" The opening statement sets the tone for the entire soliloquy, though provides a **dual meaning**. It initially seems to be a simple question about life or death, especially given the content of the soliloquy. Hamlet asks, "For who would bear the whips and scorns of time, / Th' oppressor's wrong,... When he himself might his quietus make / With a bare bodkin?" In his eyes, suicide is a real option to consider, but he notes that some people may be scared of "something after death," and so would rather "bear those ills we have" in life. However, the quote also poses a deeper philosophical question, which we'll discuss in more detail on page 48.

Hamlet then engages in a rather cruel, distasteful conversation with Ophelia. She tries to give back the gifts that he had sent her while they pined for each other. Hamlet simultaneously tells her that he loved her once and that he never loved her at all. He further goes on to say that he hates the dishonesty of beauty, and blames women for making men go crazy. This is an interesting concept, since Hamlet is unaware that Polonius is accusing Hamlet of obsessing over Ophelia as a result of his madness. It could just be very self-destructive, irrational behaviours as part of his madness "act", but at what point does his madness turn from an act to his reality?

Hamlet tells Ophelia, "Get thee to a nunnery," which once again holds dual meaning. On one hand, Hamlet is insisting that Ophelia follows through with her Christian faith in a life of chastity so that she cannot bring any other "sinners" into the world. On the other hand, Hamlet is insinuating that Ophelia should visit a brothel, due to her loose morals as a weak-minded and inferior Elizabethan woman. By extension, Hamlet is not only rejecting Ophelia in this statement, but all women in his life.

As expected, Ophelia is very disappointed with Hamlet at the conclusion of their chat. She is sad at how much Hamlet has changed, and sees that he no longer has a "noble mind." Polonius and Claudius come out from behind the tapestry. Claudius no longer believes that it was Hamlet's love for Ophelia that drove him mad. In fact, Claudius does not even believe that Hamlet has gone mad at all. In a bid to prevent any harm in the near future, Claudius wishes to send Hamlet to England, but Polonius has one last idea to get Hamlet talking. He wants to use Hamlet's trust in Gertrude to pry out the truth in a secret conversation, (though the two would spy on them the whole time). There is a return to the deceitful characteristics of Polonius and by extension, the distinct lack of trust that he displays. Claudius' final words, "Madness in great ones must not unwatched go," are slightly ironic; Claudius himself should also be watched.

Act 3 Scene 2

This scene begins with Hamlet instructing the First Player on how to perform; he requests that the player is not too passionate, but also not too tame. Effectively, Hamlet wants him to perform as if he is putting a "mirror up to nature", thus providing a reflection of reality through the play. This form of **metatheatre** draws attention towards the fictitious nature of the play, and actually challenges the play's ability to be realistic. Hamlet insists "some necessary question of the play be then to be considered," which may relate to both the question of Claudius' murderous actions, and to the larger question of life itself that Hamlet troubles himself with so often.

> Metatheatre: the theatrical device of drawing attention towards the fictitious nature of a play, and actually challenging the play's ability to be realistic.

Hamlet begins a conversation with Horatio and tells him that he is the best man that he's ever known. He believes that Horatio is "a man that Fortune's buffets and rewards / Hast ta'en with equal thanks." In other words, Horatio is someone who takes the good with the bad, and is a calm, level-headed individual. Hamlet appreciates this in Horatio because he is a voice of reason that Hamlet can trust. However, they are not necessarily character traits that Hamlet wants for himself. Instead, he is inspired by the actions of Fortinbras and the Player King, for reasons that will soon be uncovered. Hamlet reveals his trap for Claudius: "One scene of [the play] comes near the circumstance / Which I have told thee of my father's death." They are to watch Claudius carefully to determine if he is actually guilty for the murder of Old Hamlet. At this point, Hamlet is still speaking quite coherently, which supports the argument that his madness is only a façade. He is still aware enough to manipulate those around him.

The trumpets sound to signify the beginning of the play, *The Mousetrap*. The title acts as a metaphor of Hamlet's plan to trap Claudius into admitting that he killed his own brother. He's playing psychological games with Claudius, just as Claudius is trying to play with Hamlet by spying on him. Initially, Claudius tries to chat with his "cousin Hamlet" (which also means 'nephew'), but Hamlet is once again acting crazy. He tries to engage in conversation with Ophelia by using sexual innuendos and flirting with her.

However, ever the obedient daughter, she does not reciprocate much of Hamlet's attention due to her father's orders. Hamlet continues to expend his nervous, excited energy before the play starts, though he and Ophelia eventually end up on the topic of grief. He asks, "What should a man do but be merry?" However, it is somewhat ironic because he is still wearing grieving clothes four months after his father's death. This "purpose of man" that Hamlet proposes here is drastically different from his sentiments later on in the play when he truly spirals into a broken state of mind.

The play begins, and immediately, as the audience, **we can see that the events in the "play within a play" are replicating the events in *Hamlet*.** The King and the Queen are telling each other how much they love the other, but the King's death is imminent. He gives permission for the Queen to remarry, but she replies, "None wed the second but who killed the first!" Essentially, she is saying that the only people who remarry are the ones who killed their spouses in the first place.

She also implies that some other people remarry for money, but it is never for love. The King appreciates her intentions but does not believe that she'll follow through: "Purpose is but the slave to memory, / Of violent birth, but poor validity" (i.e. while she may mean what she's saying now, eventually that passion will dwindle and she'll go back on her word).

As the play continues, it is clear the Claudius and Gertrude aren't the biggest fans. Although, Hamlet reassures them that though some jokes are made in the play and that there may be "poison in jest," it's all in good fun and should not be taken seriously. He also reassures them that they should not be so concerned, because they are not guilty people; "Let the galled jade wince, our withers are unwrung." Hamlet turns to Ophelia and tries to talk to her again. She compliments his intelligence, saying that he is "keen." He makes some more lewd references towards her, about taking his "edge" off.

The play continues, and finally the revenge plot arrives. The nephew of the king "...poisons him i' th' garden for 's estate." While this definitely is a similar scenario to the supposed murder of Old Hamlet, it does have some differences. Instead of the King's brother doing the poisoning in order to take over the throne, it's the *nephew* of the king.

This foreshadows some ugly events that will unfold in a few scenes: Hamlet, Claudius' nephew, becomes a murderer when he kills Polonius, whose son, Laertes, then seeks vengeance. The play becomes a bit too much for Claudius to stomach, so he stands up and exits the hall immediately. Both Horatio and Hamlet are convinced that this means Claudius is guilty of the murder of Old Hamlet, even though they are sort of jumping to conclusions, and Claudius does not actually admit to murdering anyone at this stage.

Nevertheless, Claudius goes straight to his chambers in a bad mood. Rosencrantz and Guildenstern find Hamlet and let him know how Claudius is feeling. After all, the two men have become the King and Queen's messengers throughout the play. They let Hamlet know that Gertrude wants to speak with Hamlet alone in her bedroom (as part of Claudius and Polonius' plan to spy on Hamlet). They are still trying to figure out why Hamlet is upset. Hamlet admits, "Sir, I lack advancement, " because he believes that he has no future ahead of him. Rosencrantz and Guildenstern are confused as to why the heir to the Danish Throne would question his own future. However, Hamlet makes a cursory reference to an old proverb, "While the grass grows, the horse starves." This implies that **even if Hamlet's plans do fall into place and he catches Claudius for the murder, it might be a little too late for it to be of any use to him.**

It is at this point that Hamlet confronts the two men for spying on his actions. He asks them to play a recorder (a woodwind musical instrument), but they both refuse due to their lack of skill. Hamlet grows more frustrated, and is offended at the thought of them play him for a fool. This conversation gets cut off when Polonius enters, and urges Hamlet to visit Gertrude for a chat. Hamlet asks for a moment alone, to perform his (surprise, surprise!) fifth soliloquy of the play. It focuses on his upcoming conversation with his mother and how he wishes to conduct himself. If Hamlet's sexual conversation with Ophelia in this scene is any indication of what's to come in his chat with his mother, there are definitely some lustful undertones as part of the theme of incest that recurs in this play. Hamlet tells himself that he wants to be brutally honest with his mother, but will not cause any physical harm to her, just as the ghost asked of him. He wishes to control his emotions and "speak daggers to her," but does not (yet) want to "use" any literal daggers."

Act 3 Scene 3

Claudius begins speaking to Rosencrantz and Guildenstern, and informs them of some diplomatic business in England for which he is commissioning them. They are to go with Hamlet, because he is posing too much of a risk in Denmark. After they leave, Claudius performs a soliloquy, in which he **admits to the murder of Old Hamlet.** The audience is now certain that it was Claudius who poisoned Old Hamlet in the orchards, just as Hamlet and the players implied through *The Mousetrap*. He likens himself to Cain, who was the first murderer in the Bible. However, due to the nature of a soliloquy, Claudius is only sharing his feelings and thoughts with the audience; no other character in the play can hear what he's confessing. Claudius himself is questioning whether he can actually be forgiven for the blood on his hands because it was such a sinful action. Nevertheless, Claudius is willing to "try what repentance can" and pray.

While Claudius is kneeling in prayer, Hamlet enters the room. He contemplates murdering Claudius right then and there, but decides against it due to his religious beliefs. According to the Christian doctrine, Hamlet believes that Claudius would be allowed to enter heaven after the murder, having prayed for redemption for his sins. This does not sit well with Hamlet, because he doesn't think it's fair for Claudius to go to heaven, while his father is made to suffer in purgatory.

Metaphysical: abstract things like time, identity, mortality, or consciousness.

Hamlet has now involved himself in a problem of **metaphysical understanding**. He is distracting himself with questions of the soul, probably because he is not fully comfortable with murdering Claudius in cold blood. This is yet another **method of delay** from Hamlet, whose motives are still unclear. He has not yet been able to follow through with revenge. He got considerably close in this scene, even going so far as to pull out his sword, but once again puts it away. He wants to inflict a more radical sort of revenge. While this is not a very Christian-like thought to have, he is still only considering it due to his filial obligation for vengeance. Nevertheless, Hamlet admits "the conscience does make cowards of us all."

Act 3 Scene 4

This scene begins with Gertrude and Polonius doing some final plotting. Just before Hamlet comes to talk to his mother, Polonius hides behind the tapestry to spy on the conversation. Initially, Hamlet provides very short and bitter replies to Gertrude's questions, and is clearly distressed with her life choices lately. She starts by accusing him of being a bad son, but Hamlet soon jumps on the offensive and makes Gertrude fear for her life. She calls out for help, at which point Hamlet discovers that something is behind the tapestry. He doesn't yet realise that it is Polonius. Hamlet calls, "how now, a rat?" and stabs him through the tapestry. Both Polonius and Gertrude are shocked at the "rash and bloody deed," which ultimately leads to Polonius' death. However, Hamlet doesn't demonstrate immediate guilt for stabbing Polonius, and in fact blames Polonius for being such a busybody (i.e. "Thou find'st to be too busy is some danger"). This murder is probably one of the most disturbing moments of the entire play. His contemplation and reflection about the big questions in life are now overshadowed by this reckless behaviour and callous disregard for Polonius' life. He can no longer come across as someone with superior morals.

Gertrude is confused and distressed as to why Hamlet is being so rude to her. The audience may also be unsure of Hamlet's motives as well. It could be because Hamlet needs her support if he wants to take down Claudius. It also may be because he wants to find out if Gertrude knew about Claudius' murder of Old Hamlet. Either way, at this point it is clear that Hamlet disapproves of Gertrude's self-preservation and her remarriage, because it displays a great deal of disloyalty to Old Hamlet. He doesn't understand how she could go from loving someone that Hamlet admires greatly like Old Hamlet, to marrying someone like Claudius. He compares Old Hamlet to a Greek God, with "Hyperion curls, the front of Jove himself," whereas he says Claudius is like "a mildewed ear / Blasting his wholesome brother." Hamlet continues to accuse Gertrude of incest and adultery, bringing to the surface all of her "black and grained spots" of sins. He is disgusted that she would be in the presence of Claudius in such a sexual way; "Nay, but to live / In the rank sweat of an enseaméd med, / Stewed in corruption, honeying and making love / Over the nasty sty."

Hamlet becomes more crazed and aggressive, so much so that his words become "daggers enter[ing] [Gertrude's] ears." Still in this fragile state, Hamlet sees the ghost of Old Hamlet enter the bedroom. However, he projects his anger onto the ghost by insisting that it only showed up because Hamlet was taking too long to take revenge on Claudius. The interesting plot point in this scene is the fact that Gertrude can't actually see the ghost of her dead husband – only Hamlet can see it. She says, "This the very coinage of your brain." Thus, it is now the audience's turn to question: **is Hamlet now truly mad?** Has he been imagining the ghost and its revenge plot? Yet, Hamlet still denies that he has gone mad. He actually continues to accuse Gertrude of being a sinful being, and urges her to "confess herself to heaven". Hamlet employs an **imperative** tone with her, and makes demands of her as if he is her superior. He orders her to not "let the bloat king tempt [her] again to bed." In other words, he does not want Gertrude and Claudius to continue their incestuous actions.

Imperative: words that connote extreme importance or necessity (e.g. must, need, have to).

According to the famous psychoanalyst Sigmund Freud, this is largely a result of Hamlet's **Oedipus Complex**. Essentially, it means that Hamlet has built a strong sense of desire towards his own mother, sexually or otherwise, and as a result has developed jealousy and anger towards Claudius.

This scene provides the most substantial insight into Gertrude's character. Even though she is one of the main characters of the play, we never get a meaningful look into her thoughts or personality, because she is always in the shadow of someone else. She tries to start out in a position of power by accusing Hamlet of being disrespectful, but the more he attacks her and exposes her sins, the more submissive she becomes. This exposes her definitive goal in life: to **preserve herself and her illusion of power.** By being submissive to her husband and letting herself be seduced by Claudius, she was able to remain in a safe position. She relies on the demands of the men around her to tell her what to do and be accepted within society. This is quite evident in this scene, where she is so worn down by Hamlet's harsh words that by the end of the scene, she is asking him what to do and how to be forgiven.

Oedipus Complex: a young child's unconscious sexual desire for the parent of the opposite sex and the elimination of the other parent (according to Freud).

Act 4 Scene 1

Act 4 begins with Gertrude divulging to Claudius all the details of her conversation with Hamlet, including his murder of Polonius. She says that he is "Mad as the sea and wind when both contend / Which is the mightier." Claudius is visibly grateful that he was not hiding with Polonius behind the tapestry; otherwise he too would have been murdered. This comment demonstrates Claudius' own instincts of self-protection; he wishes to stay alive because he's living the life he always dreamed of – he has a queen, a throne and a country that he can run ambitiously. He had little to no concern for Gertrude's near-death experience, and instead considers his own wellbeing first. This is a big development of Claudius' character, as he blames himself for trying to hide Hamlet's mental condition for so long, assuming that he actually made it worse. He says, "like the owner of a foul disease, / To keep it from divulging, let it feed / Even on the pith of life."

Hamlet's madness has infected his core and drove him to murder Polonius. Gertrude still believes that there is a sliver of humanity left in Hamlet though, because he now "weeps" over having killed Polonius.

Claudius thinks that the best course of action for getting rid of the threat Hamlet poses is to follow through with the plan to send him to England. He plans to send Rosencrantz and Guildenstern with him. Once again, Claudius does this as an act of survival: "So dreaded slander... may miss our name / And hit the woundless air!" He does not want his own diplomatic reputation tarnished because of what Hamlet has done. Additionally, the fact that Gertrude tells Claudius about this murderous act demonstrates her emotional alignment to Claudius due to his position of power. While she didn't tell him that Hamlet was feigning madness, she does break Hamlet's trust by exposing him to Claudius.

Act 4 Scene 2

Hamlet finishes disposing of Polonius' body somewhere in the city of Elsinore when Rosencrantz and Guildenstern find him. They want to know what he's done with the corpse so that they can take it to the chapel, as requested by Claudius. Hamlet refuses to tell them, accusing them of being "sponges" for the King. All they want is approval from the King by doing his dirty work and finding out secrets for him. However, they're only useful when they have this secret knowledge. After they are wrung dry, they are once again disposable. Rosencrantz says that he doesn't quite understand what Hamlet is accusing them of. Hamlet replies, "A knavish speech sleeps in a foolish ear." He is convinced that the two men are too foolish to understand the "high-concept" thoughts that Hamlet has.

Self-righteous: believing oneself to be superior to others.

This demonstrates quite a **self-righteous** attitude, which is not something we have come to expect from the thoughtful Hamlet. It doesn't exactly seem that he is pretending to be mad at this point, because he appears genuinely angry. He has a biting wit and has started behaving rather impulsively. Despite being in this panic mode, Hamlet eventually agrees to go and visit the King.

Act 4 Scene 3

Heretic: someone holding beliefs that are contrary to the predominant religious doctrine, particularly Christianity.

Hamlet and Claudius finally meet in the castle, but Hamlet refuses to give Claudius any straight answers about the death of Polonius. Hamlet says that Polonius is "at supper... not where he eats, but where he is eaten," implying that Polonius is buried and being eaten by worms.

This is actually Shakespeare cleverly referencing a famous historical event called the **Diet of Worms in 1521** – a formal assembly of the Holy Roman Empire, convened with the aim to determine how authorities would respond to the teachings of Martin Luther, a prominent Protestant during the Reformation, held in Worms, Germany (hence the name). The 'Edict of Worms' was issued, which determined that should anyone find Martin Luther, he was to be denied shelter and prosecuted as a **heretic**.

Hamlet continues toying with Claudius, who is desperate to find Polonius' body. Hamlet plays **coy**, telling Claudius that if he's desperate to know, he should send a messenger to heaven. After some more sly word games, Hamlet reveals that he buried him near the stairs to the main hall. It is at this point that Claudius reveals his plans to send Hamlet away to England and makes no attempt to hide his resentment. Hamlet feigns excitement, despite the fact that he is travelling with Rosencrantz and Guildenstern, whom he does not trust at all, continuing to make maddening jokes at Claudius' expense. Claudius insists for some servicemen to follow Hamlet straight to the boat. When Claudius is finally alone, he reveals his true plans in a soliloquy. In yet another bid to protect his crown, he plans is to have Hamlet killed whilst in England. Though Hamlet is loved in Denmark, Claudius believes that it is only by those who "like not in their judgement, but their eyes". He hopes that the English King will do him this favour, since at the moment, his "joys were ne'er begun," and he will not feel secure until Hamlet is eliminated.

Coy: to act elusively or with pretend reluctance (like playing 'hard to get').

Act 4 Scene 4

Fortinbras, the young man who wishes to go to war in Poland, has finally arrived in Denmark to meet with Claudius, as per their foreign affairs agreement. Hamlet comes across the Captain of the ship, and asks him a few questions about what they're doing. The captain tells Hamlet, "Truly to speak, and with no addition, / We go to gain a little patch of ground / That hath in it no profit but the name." Essentially, the men are going to war in Poland for little to no gain in terms of land and value. Hamlet at first mocks the fact that these men are willing to spend so much time and manpower for something that doesn't really matter. However, he begins a soliloquy and his mind changes. Once again, he reflects on his own inaction in matters of revenge. Even though Hamlet arguably has a greater reason to take action, he still has been **unable to follow through with any of his plans.** On the other hand, Fortinbras and his army are clearly willing to fight "even for an eggshell." Even though Hamlet questions Fortinbras' morals, he admires the forceful nature with which he attacks everything. Nonetheless, he maintains that his "thoughts be bloody". Still, his actions haven't been as bloody as he had hoped.

Act 4 Scene 5

At the beginning of this scene, we find out that **Ophelia has gone mad** following the murder of her father, Polonius. We re-establish the motif of insanity, but this time, Ophelia has genuinely lost her mind due to external pressures that have pushed her over the edge. This is in contrast to Hamlet's 'insanity,' which was initially carried out only for Hamlet's personal gain. Ophelia is a babbling, inconsolable mess, and Gertrude is given the job of trying to talk to her. She only follows through with this task because she is trying to make up for her own sins that Hamlet has recently exposed. When Ophelia enters, she is singing about her father's death in old nursery rhyme tunes, while also mourning the loss of Hamlet. She makes some religious allusions to nomadic pilgrims, possibly in reference to Hamlet's move to England. She also makes a reference to a quote, "They say the owl was a baker's daughter." This is a popular legend in which Christ transforms a baker's daughter into an owl after the mistress denies him a piece of bread, due to the daughter's instruction. This implies that her love for both Polonius and Hamlet were somewhat **marred** by Laertes and Polonius' warnings about being virtuous, and she is now paying the price.

Mar: to be tainted or spoiled by something.

Ophelia continues singing, but now about chastity and marriage. In her song, the man had promised to marry this woman, but did not follow through with it because she had had premarital sex with him. This insinuates a possible sexual relationship between Hamlet and Ophelia, despite their religious beliefs. She soon ceases the singing, but hopes that her brother Laertes will soon avenge their dead father, because she is currently incapable.

Claudius performs a soliloquy about sorrow and guilt. He says, "When sorrow come, they come not single spies / But in battalions." He pities Ophelia, who is clearly grief-stricken due to the death of her father, the loss of Hamlet's love, and the absence of her brother. Claudius also feels bad that he hurriedly buried Polonius without a proper funeral, and is now concerned about Laertes' imminent reaction, considering he has arrived back from France and has been fed numerous rumours surrounding the circumstances of his father's death.

A messenger arrives to tell Claudius that Laertes is ready for revenge, so much so that he is leading a small rebellion with followers that want Laertes as King. Laertes enters, demanding Claudius tell him about murder of Polonius. Claudius simply tells him that he's "dead." Gertrude nervously follows, "But not by him." This is a small insight into Gertrude's **anxious, protective character.** He says, "That drop of blood that's calm proclaims me bastard, Cries "Cuckold!" to my father," announcing that he cannot be Polonius' real son if he hasn't avenged his death. This is the perfect example of Laertes and Hamlet being each other's character foils. Laertes is disgusted with himself that he hasn't avenged his father, and it's only been a matter of days. In contrast, Hamlet was visited by the ghost at the beginning of the play and has delayed the revenge plot well into the fourth act.

In another act of self-protection, Claudius insists that he had nothing to do with Polonius' murder. Laertes is willing to listen, until he sees Ophelia and things take a turn for the worse. Laertes is distraught that his sister has gone mad, and weeps at the **fragility of humanity.** He now also wants revenge for her; seeing her talk nonsense spurs him on even more. She begins to enter into a dialogue in which she uses a lot of **flower symbolism.** She uses rosemary, pansies, fennel, columbines, rues, daisies, and violets to send different messages to her family and friends. Significantly, she gives Gertrude the fennel and columbines to symbolise adultery, and gives Claudius rue symbolising regret. However, she did not give anyone violets, the flowers of faithfulness, because they are reserved for her dead father. Violets are also associated with death, because the actual flower looks like someone lowering their head in grief.

This scene highlights a dark turn in the tone of the play. Laertes is fully ready and capable of taking revenge for Polonius' murder. Not only is Claudius infected to the core with corruption, it has now infiltrated the health of the state of Denmark.

Act 4 Scene 6

This short scene involves Horatio, a servant, a sailor, and an ominous letter from Hamlet about a pirate attack. In the letter, Hamlet tells Horatio that some pirates attacked the ship he was travelling on. The pirates captured the ship and took Hamlet hostage, treating him relatively kindly considering the circumstances. He says, "They have dealt with me like thieves of mercy," and wants to reward them for doing so. The pirates were actually making their way back to Denmark. Hamlet also requests that Horatio invite the sailors in to talk to the King and Queen. Additionally, he has some information about Rosencrantz and Guildenstern that he wants to share. As per the requests, Horatio escorts the two sailors to Claudius and Gertrude, and then goes to meet with Hamlet.

Deus ex machina: an unexpected power or event that somehow saves a previously hopeless situation.

The purpose of this scene is mostly for plot development, as highlighted by the narration of the letter. The event of the pirate attack is a form of **deus ex machina**: it seems to be a bizarre reach by Shakespeare to try and resolve the issue at hand, which in this case is Hamlet's absence from the castle in Denmark.

Act 4 Scene 7

The last scene of Act 4 sees Claudius and Laertes calmly devising a revenge plot to get back at Hamlet. In trying to settle Laertes, Claudius faces his biggest challenge. Laertes' anger poses a big risk to the state of Denmark and its political stability. Initially, Laertes is confused as to why Claudius did not give Polonius a noble funeral, and why he did not punish Hamlet sufficiently. Claudius simply puts it down to two factors: firstly, Gertrude loves Hamlet too much, and he does not want to hurt her feelings.

Secondly, the Danish people also love Hamlet (partly because of his good looks). Claudius says that the public "[dips] all his faults in their affection," and implies that punishing Hamlet publicly would almost be self-sabotage. As a prideful politician, this is the last thing that Claudius would want. Laertes understands this, but is still keen to avenge his father and Ophelia now that she has gone mad.

Just as Claudius and Laertes begin discussing the plan to get back at Hamlet, the messenger enters with Hamlet's letters for the King and Queen. The letters are again used as a plot device to give some background information. It details Hamlet's travels back to Denmark and his wishes to share the story of the pirate attack in person. The fact that Hamlet is coming back actually excites Laertes, because he will be able to take immediate action in his revenge. By now, it should be very clear that Hamlet and Laertes are very different in this respect, because Hamlet has delayed his actions for a long time due to his contemplative nature.

Once the letter is read, the retribution plan really picks up some steam, as instigated by Claudius. He seems to be at the height of his scheming and deviousness, and he inspires Laertes to set up a trap. The idea is to first make spark Hamlet's jealousy about Laertes' superior swordsmanship. Hamlet will be invited to a **duel,** in which people will place bets on Hamlet to win. However, in the duel, Laertes will use a sharp knife instead of a dull one, and take it one step further by lacing the blade with a poison that will kill Hamlet instantly from any cut. If that's not enough, they put one more trap in place: if Hamlet wins the duel, he will drink from a celebratory goblet to rehydrate, but it will contain even more poison. This trap helps to kill two birds with one stone for Claudius, because he can **appease Laertes' anger** while simultaneously **getting rid of Hamlet, his ultimate threat,** once and for all. (What could go wrong!?)

During this conversation, Claudius goes on a small tangent. He highlights the importance of Laertes' urgency in this scenario by stating, "There lives within the very flame of love / A kind of wick or snuff that will abate it." Basically, he's implying that no matter how much love and passion drives Laertes' intentions now, it will eventually lose its strength and he will not follow through with his plans if he takes too long. As such, Claudius is relying on **Laertes' filial obligation to Polonius** to do him a favour and get rid of Hamlet. However, this observation is slightly ironic, and actually reflects the ideas that the Player King shared with his wife in *The Mousetrap.* Nevertheless, Laertes assures Claudius that he is going to take revenge as soon as possible, because for him, "revenge should have no bounds." He even admits that he would cut Hamlet's throat "i' th' church."

The men's discussion is again interrupted, but this time it is with the sad news that Ophelia has died. She had fallen into the water near the willow tree by reaching for some flowers. Ophelia is further associated with flowers, as she has been throughout the entire play, as a symbol of her **innocence** and **naivety.** In all of her madness, she did not understand the danger that she was in until it was too late. There are some cursory allusions to Ophelia committing suicide due to her immense grief, as evident in Act 4 Scene 5, but it is not fully clear at this point. Laertes is distressed to hear about his sister's death, which puts Claudius on edge. He is worried that Laertes is now fired up again and posing a threat to Denmark, even after Claudius spent so long trying to calm him down. However, Laertes does not cry for Ophelia. He does acknowledge that it is a normal human reaction, though subtly attributes it as a weaker, female emotion. He observes, "Nature her custom holds / Let shame say what it will." Keeping with the theme of human existence, this quote acknowledges that both Hamlet and Laertes cannot fight their instincts. Hamlet **chronically delays all of his action,** simply due to his nature, Similarly, Laertes cannot help but to take revenge for his father, because **honour and loyalty run through his veins.**

Act 5 Scene 1

Act 5 begins with two gravediggers in the churchyard preparing a plot for Ophelia's funeral. These two characters, also known as clowns in some variations of the play, are like peasants. They represent a common **archetype** from Shakespeare's plays and **provide the commoners in the Elizabethan audience someone to relate to and laugh with.** These commoners would also appreciate the **peasants' ability to outsmart the nobility in the play.** In this scene, the two gravediggers are discussing the **legitimacy of this fully Christian funeral,** considering the possibility that Ophelia actually committed suicide and did not die accidentally. In the Christian doctrine, this would mean she should not be honoured with such a funeral, but the gravediggers observe that she is getting this special treatment because she lived in a rich family. Throughout the chat, the two gravediggers make a lot of jokes and engage in a lot of word play, which adds some light to the quite macabre atmosphere and circumstances of her death.

> **Archetype:** a typical or perfect example of something.

They also try to demonstrate the honour of being a gravedigger, likening their profession to the works of Adam in the Bible. They believe that their profession is necessary, and more important than that of "mason[s], shipwright[s], or carpenter[s]" because their graves will last longer than any building.

Hamlet and Horatio enter the scene. Hamlet sees the gravediggers from afar, and is shocked at their ability to sing and make jokes while carrying out such a dark task. However, he understands that it is their job and they are somewhat desensitised to death. The gravediggers begin tossing around a skull. Hamlet gives it a voice due to his emotional connection and contemplation about existence. He says, "that skull had a tongue in it and could sing once." It is clear that Hamlet now is not only concerned about the **spirit of people once they die,** but also obsessed with the **physicality of death** – what happens to the body once the person dies? This was also addressed with the allusion to the Diet of Worms after he murdered Polonius (see page 22).

Hamlet then tried to find out whose grave it actually is. However, he gets irritated when they refuse to give him a straight answer. Instead, they play word games with him. They get onto the topic of the 'crazy' prince Hamlet, who was shipped of to England because he had gone insane (the gravediggers are obviously unaware that they are actually talking to Hamlet). Hamlet then sees the skull that the two men were playing with, and somehow realises that it is actually the skull of Yorick, the old court jester from Hamlet's childhood who has been dead for 23 years. He gets quite worked up about seeing Yorick, referencing his lips and his skin that no longer exist. This is another instance of Hamlet's **fascination with the physical reality of death.** Hamlet makes an **historical allusion** to Alexander the Great, who even though he was a successful man in his life, he now "returneth to dust."

Following this revelation, Claudius, Gertrude, Laertes, and a priest enter the scene carrying Ophelia in a coffin. Laertes insists that the Priest perform every burial rite possible to honour his sister, even though her death was under suspicious circumstances, but the priest does not want to dishonour the other deceased individuals. Laertes is still clearly distressed about Ophelia's death, and only wants the best for her: "Lay her i' th' earth, / And from her fair and unpolluted flesh / May violets spring!" Ophelia is again associated with flowers, chastity and innocence, yet there seem to be some subtle undertones of incest between Laertes and Ophelia in this scene, aligned with the subtle undertones between Gertrude and Hamlet.

It is at this time that Hamlet finds out about Ophelia's death, which visibly distresses him as well. However, Laertes is still livid with Hamlet for causing this mess, though Hamlet does not admit any guilt for the death of Ophelia, even though Polonius' murder was a major contributing factor in Ophelia's downward spiral, and this was *definitely* Hamlet's fault! Nevertheless, Hamlet and Laertes both insist that they are willing to sacrifice anything for Ophelia. This leads to a small wrestling match between the two, but is abruptly stopped. Hamlet then actually admits that he loved Ophelia, despite telling her the opposite when she was alive. Gertrude and Claudius just dismiss Hamlet's dialogue as insanity. At the end of the scene, Claudius reasserts the revenge plan to Laertes, but implores him to be patient.

Act 5 Scene 2

In the final scene of the play, a lot of action takes place and a lot of loose ends are tied up. We begin with Hamlet sharing his story with Horatio that he had promised in his letter. Hamlet had found out that Claudius only sent him to England for him to be immediately executed. To rectify this, Hamlet forged a new note on behalf of the Royal Danish family, which instead ordered for Rosencrantz and Guildenstern's deaths. Hamlet feels no guilt for this, and believes that the two men got what they deserved. As a result of this, Hamlet is confident that it is time to take revenge on Claudius and get rid of him once and for all.

Just as Hamlet is about to share some form of guilt about Laertes, a young courtier called Osric enters. He comes to inform Hamlet about the fencing duel planned by Claudius and Laertes. The courtier speaks very vaguely and in a roundabout manner, which Hamlet actually mocks in his own speech. This makes it somewhat difficult to decipher what the two men are talking about. Hamlet believes that there is no substance behind Osric's words, as indicated by, "and do but blow them to their trial, the bubbles are out." The two men continue chatting, and start praising Laertes' fencing skills. However, for this bet, he has been handicapped; he must win by at least three strikes. The stakes are quite high, with plenty of weapons on the line. As part of the plan, Claudius has bet on Hamlet to win so that he is enticed to compete. Horatio tries to advise Hamlet not to compete because he doesn't think that he stands a chance, but Hamlet simply believes in God's plan and destiny. He states, "if it be now, 'tis not to come. If it be not to come, it will be now." So, Hamlet agrees to take part in the duel. A messenger arrives to signal the initiation of the duel, but informs Hamlet that his mother wishes him to speak nicely to Laertes before they start. It is possible that Gertrude is trying to display some form of loyalty towards Hamlet as her beloved son, but won't do so in public. She doesn't want to ruin her reputation or put her own safety at risk.

Claudius, Gertrude, and Laertes now enter the hall. Laertes and Hamlet shake hands as a sign of respect, even though it's not fully genuine. At this point, **Hamlet demonstrates a stark change in character,** possibly due to his mother's instruction. He vaguely **apologises to Laertes for murdering Polonius, but distances himself from the guilt by blaming his mental illness.** He says, "if Hamlet from himself be ta'en away ,/ And when he's not himself does wrong Laertes, / Then Hamlet does it not. Hamlet denies it. / Who does it, then? His madness." His third person speech is a bizarre subversion from the first person narrative that he used throughout the whole play. However, what's interesting here is that for the whole play, Hamlet was adamant that he was not actually going mad, and was only pretending, as is typical of Hamlet's **self-contradictory personality.** He makes himself **the victim of his own mental illness, rather than admitting to the horrors of cold-blooded murder.** Nevertheless, this demonstration of sympathy for Laertes is a big change for Hamlet, who almost seems at peace with what he's done. Laertes does actually accept this confession, saying that he "receive[s] [Hamlet's] love like love." However, unlike Hamlet, Laertes is still prepared to fight honourably in his father's name.

Claudius announces the rules of the duel, and the fighting begins. He emphasises the fact that, should Hamlet win, **he would take a celebratory drink from a goblet.** At first, Hamlet takes a couple of successful jabs at Laertes. In celebration, Claudius prepares the drink, spiking it with a poison pearl, but Hamlet doesn't actually drink it straight away. Instead, Gertrude has a sip of the poisoned drink. Suddenly, Laertes strikes and makes his move to stab Hamlet with his extra sharp sword. He wounds Hamlet, but in the ensuing commotion, Hamlet takes Laertes' poisoned sword, eventually wounding Laertes with the poisoned weapon. At this point, Gertrude, Laertes, and Hamlet have all been poisoned in some way. Gertrude collapses and out of guilt, Laertes reveals his revenge plot. He feels like "a woodcock to mine own springe" or like **a mouse in his own trap** (a reference to the earlier play-within-a-play, *The Mousetrap,* which acts as an allegory for *Hamlet*). Though Laertes admits to the plot, he actually blames Claudius for devising it. As a result, Hamlet launches for Claudius, wounds him and force-feeds him the poisoned drink. This ultimately leads to Claudius' death. Hamlet **finally gets his revenge,** even though he was somewhat forced into doing it.

Just before Laertes dies, he tells Hamlet that he forgives him for what he did to Polonius and Ophelia, and asks for forgiveness from Hamlet for poisoning him. Then, it's Hamlet's turn to die. In his final words, **he wishes that Horatio would retell the story of Hamlet's glorious life.** Though Horatio considers poisoning himself, he chooses to follow through with his best friends wishes, and not commit the sin of suicide. After such a slow and dizzying build up to the climax, the death of most of the main characters comes very quickly via **regicide**. **It ties together the themes of revenge and justice very neatly, with most individuals being able to exact their revenge before their death.**

Regicide: the act of killing a king.

Immediately following the chaos, Prince Fortinbras and the English ambassador visit the castle. They are confused by all the death, but Horatio promises that he will share the stories of the Danish court. Horatio wants the men to be honoured in their death because of their great contributions. This transition back into politics brings the story back to reality, without all the scheming and corruption. Fortinbras actually seems to be a much more **strong-willed and capable leader than Claudius was or Hamlet could have been,** thus providing some hope for the future. The English ambassador informs Horatio that, as per the King's wishes, Rosencrantz and Guildenstern were executed. Comparatively, Fortinbras arrived to inform the King that he had successfully conquered the desired land in Poland. However, now that no one is left in the Danish court, Fortinbras wishes to take claim of Denmark. Horatio informs Fortinbras that Hamlet supports Fortinbras in that endeavour; Hamlet had said so just before he died. As evident throughout the play, Hamlet greatly admired Fortinbras' bravery and ability to action. Some cannons fire, finally signifying the end of the play.

Section 4

Character Analysis

Hamlet

Hamlet, Prince of Denmark, is the **central character** of this Shakespearean tragedy. He is the son of the recently murdered King Hamlet, and of Queen Gertrude. While he was away studying at Wittenberg University, his uncle Claudius had hastily married Gertrude to become King of Denmark.

Primarily, Hamlet is grieving the loss of his father and the betrayal of his immoral mother remarrying so quickly. As a result, he does not support the political or familial decisions made by Claudius, though this leads to his estrangement within the court. This is particularly difficult due to Hamlet's budding relationship with Ophelia. Things are made even more difficult when Hamlet encounters the spirit of his father, King Hamlet. He appears as a ghost to inform Hamlet of his murder at the hands of Claudius. King Hamlet calls for revenge to be taken in his honour, and this is where a lot of the emotional problems begin for Hamlet. Already grieving, he is now confused as to if or how he should exact this revenge, based on his **filial obligation** to his father and his initial inability to prove Claudius' guilt. This crisis highlights Hamlet's **contradictory** personality traits.

Originally **cynical, existential,** and **bitter, madness** eventually creeps in and wreaks havoc in Hamlet's life. He obsesses over this revenge plot but can never quite follow through with his plans. However, his delay begins to infuriate him because, unlike the characters that he admires (such as Fortinbras), he cannot act boldly. He is stuck within his own mortal contemplations about life and philosophy. However, his reflective nature does at times spark him to make brash decisions, especially at the height of his perceived madness, as can be seen in the murder of Polonius.

As the drama unfolds, we see that **Hamlet's insane actions are actually threatening the state of Denmark, and by extension, King Claudius himself.** His further refusal to work with Claudius and his emotional shut down towards Gertrude leads to further **corruption** within the court. Ultimately, Hamlet's untimely death in the final scene of the play may have come as a sweet release after the constant mental battles that he experienced during his grieving process. Nevertheless, Hamlet's search for truth is the driving force behind the play.

> **Existentialism**: a philosophical theory that emphasises an individual's existence, and how that individual is free to be responsible for their own development through their wilful actions.

Claudius

Claudius becomes the King of Denmark following the death of King Hamlet, his brother. He marries Queen Gertrude, even though he is her brother-in-law and Hamlet's uncle. Claudius is the villain of the play; he is manipulative, ambitious and not afraid to take action against anyone that he considers a threat to his throne, even if it means murder. According to the ghost who speaks to Hamlet, Claudius is responsible for poisoning King Hamlet for his own gain and deserves to be **castigated**. Throughout the play, Claudius can't quite work out Hamlet's motives and the reasons for his apparent insanity. Although, he immediately understands that Hamlet poses a threat to his throne, since he is the son of the now-dead King. Claudius is mostly cold and calculating, though does seem to display genuine emotion toward his new wife, Gertrude. Otherwise, most other characters in the court are disposable to him.

Castigate: punished or severely rebuked and reprimanded for an offence.

Gertrude

Gertrude is the Queen of Denmark, Hamlet's mother, and now Claudius' wife. We do not get to see her on her own in any scenes, or hear her thoughts via any **monologues** throughout the play, so **we do not get a clear view of her perspective, unlike many other main characters.** This makes her one of the most mysterious figures in the play. She does demonstrate great deal of love for her son, Hamlet, but he thinks that she is simply a weak-minded, overly emotional woman. He accuses her of being lustful due to her hasty marriage to Claudius, which contradicts his expectations of her as an Elizabethan woman. She experiences some verbal abuse from Hamlet about remaining uncorrupted as a result. It is reasonable to assume that Gertrude complies with a lot of the demands asked of her due to her **distinct need for self-preservation; she will do anything to stay safe and feel needed.**

Monologue: a long speech by one character within a conversation.

Self-preservation: the human instinct to survive.

Polonius

Polonius is **Claudius' right-hand man.** He is the Lord Chamberlain of the Danish court, so he is in charge of supervising all the household departments, advising and communicating with the King and his kingdom. He is the father of Laertes and Ophelia, and though he shows good intentions to take care of them, it does not always translate well. He seems to be overprotective of his family, and the issues of Claudius (whose issues are, in turn, issues of Denmark), though does whatever he can for the greater good. However, there is definitely more to Polonius than meets the eye. He does a lot of things in secret and as such demonstrates significant **distrust** in his children. This leads to him jumping to a lot of incorrect conclusions. He also is deceptive in his actions toward Hamlet, such as when he spied on Hamlet and Gertrude's conversation for Claudius' benefit. Though, for the duration of the play he can never quite figure out what Hamlet is up to. Meanwhile, Polonius camouflages his somewhat manipulative actions through long and comical rants, which redirects audiences to believe that he is just a man motivated by his care for his children and his country.

Ophelia

Ophelia is Polonius' daughter and **Hamlet's love interest**. She embodies the **archetypal Elizabethan womanly values of chastity, obedience, and silence** by being submissive to her father and brother's demands. The sweet, innocent girl gets caught up in Polonius' deceitful plans of spying on Hamlet. She heavily relies on her father's direction, but **once he is murdered by Hamlet, she spirals into insanity.** Her façade of compliance falls when she begins to expose the sexually exploitative nature of the men in her life who had controlled her actions. **Her madness actually parallels that of Hamlet,** both of whom are drawn into psychological turmoil by their grief. In her final moments, Ophelia sings and uses flowers as symbols to condemn Claudius and Gertrude's actions. Mentally and emotionally drained, she ultimately drowns and dies in Act IV Scene VII. It is possible that she committed suicide because of her father's recent murder and her rejection from Hamlet, as her naïve nature may not have allowed her to deal with solitude effectively. However, it is also possible that she was insane to the point that she did not understand the danger that she was in; reality was no longer clear for her.

> **Archetypal:** a very typical example of a character and their behaviours. Similar to stereotypes.

Laertes

Laertes is the son of Polonius and brother of Ophelia. For the majority of the play, he is off in France studying with an expert swordsman. However, when he hears of his father's death, he storms back to Denmark to exact revenge upon his father's murderer, even though he is not overly emotional or distraught like his sister, Ophelia. **Laertes is a foil for Hamlet, due to his rash decision-making and immediate action.** In contrast, Hamlet is largely contemplative and delays his revenge because he is unsure of the truth. Additionally, many similarities can be drawn in the character development of both Hamlet and Laertes. Both have their fathers murdered, and lose people who are very close to them over the course of the play, though, Laertes' passion ultimately forces him to let loose a lot faster than the agonised, grieving Hamlet. Laertes' final revenge plot to kill Hamlet is greatly instigated by Claudius, who encourages him to use similar poisonous techniques that caused the murder of King Hamlet in the first place. In the end, Laertes dies trying to avenge his father's death and protect the family name.

The Ghost

The ghost is the **apparition of King Hamlet's spirit**, poisoned by King Claudius. He only speaks to Hamlet, informing him of the murder and encouraging him to take revenge on Claudius on his behalf. It becomes a significant moral dilemma for Hamlet, who is never completely sure that taking revenge is the right thing to do. As a result, the ghost becomes a **symbol of confusion and is the physical manifestation of Hamlet's insanity.** Hamlet is not even sure that the ghost is real, and speculates that it might be an evil spirit sent to disturb him. More significantly, due to the fact that Gertrude cannot see the ghost when she and Hamlet are arguing, it is possible that the ghost is simply a figment of Hamlet's vivid imagination as he grieves for the death of his father. This question is never properly answered, but ultimately the ghost is the instigator of most of the chaos in the play.

Horatio

Horatio is Hamlet's best friend and schoolmate from Wittenberg University. He is Hamlet's most trusted and loyal friend, and actually remains that way throughout the duration of the play, amidst all the chaos. He acts as a moral guide and a voice of reason for Hamlet, by using evidence and logic to draw conclusions. His trustworthiness and **equanimity** is established as early as the first scene in the play; he reasonably denies the existence of the ghost, until he sees it with his own eyes. At that point, he becomes justifiably scared and cautious of the events to come. Hamlet admires Horatio's level-headedness, though has a completely different attitude towards life. Horatio is one of the few characters that survives the conclusion of the play – which can be seen as Shakespeare's subtle endorsement of Horatio's worldview – and so lives to tell the story of Hamlet and the Danish court.

Equanimity: calmness and composure, especially in a difficult situation.

Fortinbras

Similarly to Hamlet, Fortinbras is the young prince of Norway whose father was killed. Old Hamlet murdered King Fortinbras on the battlefield thirty years before this play begins, and as a result, the Norwegian throne was given to Fortinbras' uncle. Fortinbras has his own desires for revenge; he intends to attack Denmark and reclaim some land for Norway in order to avenge his father. He has a **brash** and **impetuous** nature, and often turns to military actions to seek justice and honour (in fact, his name actually translates to "strong in arm"). However, the King of Norway is initially upset with his nephew's rapid decision to wage war. Claudius then sends Voltimand and Cornelius, two courtiers, to make an agreement with the Norwegian King. Claudius guarantees Norway a safe passage through Denmark, so that Fortinbras can instead take some land from Poland. Fortinbras is absent for the majority of the play because he is out fighting this war. However, in the final scene, he arrives back to Denmark following his victory in Poland, only to find that the entire Danish royal family has been murdered. He ultimately takes the Danish land as well for the Norwegian kingdom.

Rosencrantz and Guildenstern

Rosencrantz and Guildenstern are Hamlet's schoolmates from Wittenberg University. Their main role, as prompted by Claudius and Gertrude, is to find out why Hamlet has gone mad. They are somewhat **enigmatic** throughout the play, and it seems as though Hamlet himself cannot differentiate them. He always addresses them as a pair, and they essentially play the same role. While they are trying to figure out what is wrong with Hamlet, they continuously question him. This is a parody of a Socratic dialogue, whereby a 'question and answer' method is employed to discuss moral and philosophical problems. However, Hamlet does not always cooperate with them in this respect. Ultimately, their commissioning to spy on Hamlet ultimately leads to their death. Hamlet discovers their betrayal and orders for their execution in England instead of his.

> **Enigmatic:** difficult to interpret or understand.

Minor characters

The Players

The Players are the group of actors who come to Denmark to perform to the court. Though the relationships with the individual characters are somewhat insignificant, they still play a pivotal role in exposing Claudius' murder of King Hamlet. Shakespeare has Hamlet use the players in their play, *The Mousetrap*, to echo the events of his overarching play, as their performance is rife with similarities, including the death of a monarch and a thick revenge plot.

Marcellus and Barnardo

These two guards are the first people to witness the ghost of King Hamlet. They alert Horatio, who then convinces Hamlet to stand guard and bear witness. The fact that they witness the ghost validates its appearance, and in turn, Hamlet's state of mind.

Francisco and Reynaldo

Francisco is a soldier at Elsinore, Denmark. Reynaldo is Polonius' servant, who is sent to France to spy on Polonius' son, Laertes. It is actions like these that make Polonius seem deceitful and distrusting in his relationships.

Gravediggers

The gravediggers are present following the death of Ophelia. Hamlet finds them while they are digging her grave, and engages in a slightly irritating conversation filled with puns and attempted comedy. It is at this time that Hamlet has yet another **existential crisis.** He finds **Yorick's skull,** which is a universally recognisable symbol of *Hamlet*. The sight of Yorick, the former court jester, and the tangible proof of his death, leads Hamlet to question his own mortality.

# Section 5

Key Themes Analysis

There are many recurring themes in *Hamlet* that you can use to organise your essays. There are also some great resources online if you wish to do some more research on these key themes, or on different readings of the play to help you demonstrate to your markers that you've done your own research and know what you're talking about!

Revenge

The theme of revenge is very clear throughout the entire play, and is perhaps the most prominent of all the themes since this is a 'revenge tragedy.' Most significantly, Hamlet, Laertes, and Fortinbras are all tasked with revenge, though they carry out their duties in very different ways. They are all driven by their **filial obligations** – that is, the services and actions that children must provide for their parents out of respect and honour. For example, it is immediately established by the ghost that Hamlet must avenge his father's murder. However, throughout the play it is evident that **the revenge plots put in place are quite damaging to the mental and physical health of the individuals. It can eventually lead to moral degradation, obsessive behaviours, and death.**

There are some pretty good contextual links to the revenge theme, which will help broaden your understanding of the characters' motivations to get revenge. Before and during the Elizabethan era, there were very basic concerns about an individual's relationship to the state, as well as getting justice through violent or legal means. While many places were self-governed by powerful families, **blood feuds** were a very prominent feature in society. This involved long-running arguments or fights between families, especially if one family tried to take revenge for the actions inflicted by the other family.

Additionally, many people felt that it was justified to take justice into their own hands instead of leaving it to law enforcement – they wanted the punishment to fit the crime as they saw it. This is explored throughout the play as Hamlet deals with the corruption of the Danish court. His anger towards Claudius increases, not only for this corruption, but also as part of his own filial obligation. This ultimately ends in violent revenge.

Another contextual link to revenge is Christianity. Considering the strong allegorical links to Christianity, there is a lot of violence that takes place in the play. Instead of embarking on individual revenge quests, Shakespeare endorses the notion that **people should leave justice and retribution to God,** because it is his job according to religious doctrine. Hence, the characters who instead choose to pursue their own revenge at any cost are the ones who end up dead by the play's end.

This play also follows a particular dramatic structure, which further emphasises the theme of revenge. **Freytag's Tragedy Structure** can be identified as follows:

1. The establishment of a tragedy that **requires revenge** (i.e. Old Hamlet's murder, and Hamlet's filial obligation to get revenge).
2. The revenge plot acts as a **catalyst for the gradual moral corruption of the main character** (i.e. Hamlet's gradual insanity, the murder of Polonius, and ordering Rosencrantz and Guildenstern's deaths, amongst other things).
3. Eventually, the revenge plot builds up to a **climax in which the main character and many other major characters die** (i.e. the final duel between Hamlet and Laertes, wherein Claudius, Gertrude, Laertes, and Hamlet all die in Act 5 Scene 2).

As aforementioned, revenge is represented through the characterisations of Hamlet, Laertes, and Fortinbras. Hamlet is initially depicted as an **amicable** and charming man. Claudius addresses the fact that the people of Denmark really like Hamlet, which prevents him from eliminating Hamlet as a threat. However, Hamlet's morals degrade more and more as he obsesses over revenge, despite his religious beliefs. His ethical and moral corruption is clearly evident when he murders Polonius in cold blood, though at least in this situation, he shows a little bit of remorse by weeping. By contrast, when he signs the death letter for Rosencrantz and Guildenstern, he merely blames them for being weak. Evidently, **the more that Hamlet delays his revenge and becomes preoccupied with it, the more morally corrupt he becomes.** When he finally stabs Claudius and fulfils his obligation to his father, he immediately looks for balance in the world. However, even when Hamlet does murder Claudius, he receives some form of sympathy from the audience, because he delayed it for so long. It seems as though he had a hard time coming face to face with his revenge plot, because he used to be such an admirable man.

Amicable: friendly and good-natured.

In comparison, Laertes has no problem putting his revenge into action because of his **reckless nature.** However, it is this unruliness that ultimately corrupts him and leads to his death. Like Hamlet, Laertes was originally a noble and good character. But, with growing political power and people rallying behind him to take revenge after his father's murder (as evident in Act 4 Scene 5), Laertes was inspired to take action immediately. This obligation increased his moral degradation, as symbolised by a change in his tone and a more aggressive dialogue. He even admits that he would cut Hamlet's throat "i' th' church." In the end, Laertes dies because of this rage and desire to avenge his father. **Dramatic irony** is used in this sense, as Laertes' revenge plot actually backfired on him when his own poisoned sword was used to would him. It highlights the **consequences of revenge.**

Dramatic irony: when a play's audience is aware of something that its characters are not.

Fortinbras has a different attitude towards revenge and as such is rewarded for allowing God and nature to balance out any bad deeds. Fortinbras feels obligated to go to war due to his father's loss in battle, however he is **diplomatic enough to listen to advice from his superiors.** He respects his uncle's wishes, even though he is eager to take action. This willingness juxtaposes Hamlet's chronic delay and eventual moral corruption. As he doesn't give in to the revenge plot, Fortinbras is rewarded with Norway, Denmark, and Poland, whereas Hamlet is punished with death by poison.

Appearance and reality

> **Subjective framework:** the contextual influences – social, historical, emotional – that influence an author's perspective and by extension, their writing.

In *Hamlet* there is a very hazy distinction between **how things appear and how they actually are.** Many characters act with some pretense, or in some way conceal their truth, making it difficult to determine what's real. This trickery escalates into madness for many of the characters in the play. When analysing the effects of this blurring between appearance and reality on the characters, it's important to consider their **subjective framework.**

First, we must acknowledge the philosophical shift from Renaissance Humanism to Sceptical Humanism (as explored on page 4). While Renaissance Humanism encouraged mankind to expand its wealth of knowledge, **Sceptical Humanism instead focused on the unobtainability of such certainties and abstract ideas in life.** The character of Hamlet represents these struggles. He is faced with the difficult task of **rectifying an injustice that he is never actually sure of** – that is, the murder of his father at the hands of Claudius. Even though Hamlet does ask some "big questions" about life, death, and the nature of existence, he also addresses the difficulty of understanding the truth about other people. It is difficult to navigate the facts of guilt or innocence, sanity or insanity, if the truth is not as it seems. Essentially, the entire world, even our modern society, is filled with contradictions between appearance and reality. This play demonstrates the struggles of trying to navigate such a world.

A really key symbol of this thematic concern is the Ghost of Old Hamlet. Based on the Elizabethan Christian context, the ghost symbolises an unnatural disturbance to the natural balance of society. This makes the audience immediately unsure of the intentions of the ghost: are they genuine? Or does he only exist to disturb the balance in Denmark? This is established in the Ghost's request of Hamlet to take revenge upon "the smiling, damned villain" (Claudius) and let Gertrude, the "pernicious woman", suffer. Already he is encouraging Hamlet to fulfil the difficult task of wearing a mask and being deceitful. However, Hamlet feels ill-equipped for this job because it is his priority to find truth, not lies.

In the end, **the ghost becomes a physical manifestation of Hamlet's insanity** that has worsened as a result of his search for truth. That Gertrude cannot see the ghost in Act 3 Scene 4, despite Hamlet being adamant that it was in the room, makes the audiences question if Hamlet is even pretending to be mad by that point.

Additionally, we have to look at the **dramatic structure** and its influence on the appearances and realities in *Hamlet,* and how it allows characters to sustain their **'masks.'** Based on the nature of soliloquies and asides, the character that is speaking can announce their truth or think aloud, but the other characters in the play cannot hear. Hence, they can still act in duplicitous ways around their friends and family, but they **break the fourth wall** and inform the audience of their true thoughts.

This can be seen in Hamlet's first soliloquy in which he decides to put on an "antic disposition" and make everyone believe that he's gone mad. Claudius also takes off his metaphorical mask when he announces in his soliloquy that he shipped Hamlet off to England to get executed in secret in Act 3 Scene 3.

There are many more instances of acting and the use of masks within the play beyond this, which causes Hamlet to lose control at times. He is visibly frustrated at how easy it is for others to conceal the truth. Claudius, the corrupt politician, wears a mask of generosity and benevolence to be in the public's good books, but Hamlet identifies him as someone who "may smile and smile and be a villain."

Hamlet also expresses significant distress towards women and their 'masks.' Though he directs his anger towards Ophelia, his old love, it is more a **misogynistic** comment on Elizabethan women collectively. He dislikes their physical mask of makeup, which he calls "painting," and is angered how "God hath given [women] one face" and yet they "make [themselves] another." However, in regards to Ophelia, once her mask deteriorates and her madness is exposed (following the murder of Polonius), she begins to speak the truth more freely. Even though she becomes "divided from herself and her fair judgement," she still thinks coherently enough to use flowers as symbolism for the lives of others. This is evident in her giving Claudius fennel and columbine to symbolise adultery and faithlessness.

In stark contrast, many people appreciate the character of Horatio, because he does not use a mask. He is loyal and faithful to his friend Hamlet throughout the whole play, and acts as a moral guide. He is rewarded with trust from Hamlet due to his clarity in personality and actions, and can be said to have been rewarded by Shakespeare in escaping the final act of the play with his life.

Break the fourth wall: when a character seems aware of their own existence within a play. The fourth wall is an imaginary wall that exists between actors and the audience.

Mortality, humanity, and fate

The interconnecting themes of mortality, humanity, and fate all relate to Hamlet's perception of the **human experience,** which further highlights his internal conflicts. The tone of *Hamlet* is very **existential,** especially Hamlet's dialogue. He is stricken with grief due to his father's death and develops a sense of ennui. As a result, he begins to question his existence, as seen in the "to be or not to be" soliloquy. Hamlet is asking whether to live or die, but also is considering a more abstract concept of life and death, influenced by Shakespeare's subjective framework of Renaissance Humanism. This is exacerbated with his discovery of Yorick's skull; he tries to give a voice to the skull and personify it, but ultimately it is futile. After all, everyone, no matter if they're nobility or a commoner, ends up in the same place. When Hamlet draws this conclusion, **it is at the height of his madness during which the most resonant truths are exposed.**

> **Ennui:** feeling of boredom or dissatisfaction.
>
> **Resonant:** in this context, something that stands out as meaningful to the audience.

Throughout the play, Hamlet is conflicted between **fate and the power of humanity.** In this sense, fate has strong religious connotations; it is the course of events over an individual's lifetime, predetermined by God. Fate is often used in tragedies as a result of an 'unbalanced' natural order and unnatural acts.

Initially, Hamlet regrets being tasked with revenge as part of his destiny. He acknowledges he things of himself as having been "born to set [the world] right," but as the play progresses and his sanity spirals, he simply takes destiny on board as a fact of life. This is because of his internal battle between believing in fate and believing in humanist values. Contrary to fate, humanists value the fact that we are people capable of reason and error, ultimately making our own decisions in life. The philosophy also encourages a search for the self, which is central in *Hamlet*. The **first piece of dialogue** by Bernardo, "Who's there?" already asks the overarching questions about humanity in a subtle, figurative way. We also explore the many faces of humanity. Similarly to the metaphorical masks, we witness both the **bestial and intellectual facets of human nature,** because we are "crawling between earth and heaven." Unfortunately, corruption can also implicate the lives of others, who end up suffering for other people's sins or actions, as demonstrated by Ophelia's descent into madness following her father's murder.

It is a difficult task for Hamlet to decide between fate and self-determination throughout the entire play. However, when the masks drop and madness prevails, Hamlet finally finds some sort of end to his dilemma. He discovers that we as **humans are only mortal; no matter what happens in life, we all end up in the same place at the end.** He doesn't want this harsh, existential discovery to be in vain because it caused him such emotional turmoil. That is why he insists that Horatio carries on in life; he trusts his friend to live "to tell [his] story."

Religion

As you can probably tell by now, religion plays a large role in *Hamlet*, both through the actions of the characters, as well as the way in which Elizabethan beliefs and philosophies influenced Shakespeare's writing (i.e. in a metatheatrical way). Events such as the Reformation of 1517 would have significantly dictated *Hamlet's* storytelling. Most significantly, Shakespeare demonstrates a disparity between King Hamlet and Prince Hamlet's religious beliefs. It is implied that King Hamlet is Catholic, because he died without being forgiven for his sins, and was sent to purgatory as a consequence. However, with Elizabethan English citizens being mandated to join the Protestant church, we see signs that imply that Prince Hamlet is Protestant (unlike his father). Hamlet actually attends Wittenberg University, which was a real university formed by Martin Luther, a very prominent reformer. As a result of their differing beliefs, some internal and external conflict is created with the appearance of the ghost from purgatory. It is this confusion that fuels Hamlet's contemplation, madness and his **self-perpetuating** inaction over the course of the play.

Self-perpetuating: something that forces itself to grow or continue, and is able to keep going without external influence.

Women and sex

Throughout the play, Hamlet demonstrates an intense preoccupation with women and their seemingly weak control over emotions (as per the Elizabethan **subjective framework**). Within Shakespeare's context, there were a lot of enforced stereotypes, including the roles of women in society. Women were expected to be domestic and submissive, and experienced prejudice as the 'inferior' sex. Hamlet feels **betrayed by the women in his life,** namely Gertrude through her marriage to Claudius, and Ophelia through her rejection of Hamlet's love. It is worth noting that both Gertrude and Ophelia's betrayals were as a result of self-preservation and obedience, which was the typical behaviour expected of Elizabethan women. As a result, Hamlet lost his faith in women and tried very hard to reinforce the female stereotypes. His imperative demand to Ophelia, "Get three to a nunnery," underscores his view that the only legitimate roles of women in society are either chaste lives like nuns, or lustful, sinful lives like brothel workers.

Even when Hamlet kills Polonius accidentally, he turns straight to Gertrude to make sure that she does not betray him as she has in the past with her "incestuous" marriage. He doesn't even go to Claudius to exact his real revenge plot. He goes to chastise Gertrude about her sexual relationship with Claudius, her ex-brother-in-law. The conversation between Gertrude and Hamlet demonstrates its own incestuous undertones, which has been explored by different directors and actors through history. For example, director Laurence Olivier directed a 1948 film directly based on Shakespeare's *Hamlet*. Although, in this scene, he greatly exaggerates Gertrude and Hamlet's relationship, to the extent that it makes audiences quite uncomfortable.

Look out for other film adaptations, appropriations or modern stage productions of Hamlet, as they help to demonstrate the play's **textual integrity.** This can be great to include in your essay, even as a cursory reference, as it adds depth to your analysis and can even help you to develop your own opinions and theories about character motivations.

While Hamlet and Old Hamlet consider the relationship between Gertrude and Claudius to contribute to the "national pollution" in Denmark, no one else actually addresses it as an issue. This may be because incest is a universal taboo, and Gertrude and Claudius do not want to admit to it. For example, Claudius apologises for committing fratricide, but never apologises for his hasty marriage to Gertrude. Similarly, Hamlet is the only one who blames Gertrude for being lustful and allowing herself to be seduced by Claudius. However, it could also be because no one else really sees problem with it; Old Hamlet and Hamlet seem to be the only ones who take issue with their relationship, probably because they feel betrayed by the main woman in their lives. In addition, some variations of *Hamlet* hint at an incestuous relationship between Laertes and Ophelia, especially due to his dominating tone, her submission, and his display of love and acts of despair following her death.

Surveillance and trust

Conceit: a recurring metaphor or trope.

As aforementioned, *Hamlet* is filled with deception and distinct distrust between characters, as evident by the significant degree of surveillance. The **conceit** of spying and mistrust is established in the very first line of the first scene. Bernardo rhetorically asks, "Who's there?" while he is on guard and is surveying the castle grounds. This is also emphasised due to the play starting in medias res. This is only the start of a recurring surveillance motif through the entire play. One character that epitomises this theme is Polonius. While he initially gives off the vibe of an overprotective father, it is soon revealed that he does not trust his children or the people of the Danish court. He gives the illusion that he trusts Laertes on his trip to France, but then sends a courtier to go and spy on him. This does demonstrate Polonius' filial duty to take care of Laertes, which is honourable in some respect. However, it is this lack of trust and incessant spying that ultimately leads to Polonius' downfall, both literally and metaphorically, as he was spying on Hamlet from behind a tapestry when Hamlet stabbed him, but it was his mistrust that spurred him to pursue such actions in the first place.

There are some other characters that display trust issues and engage in espionage because of their contextual obligation to the king. The **Divine Right of Kings** suggests that the monarch is all-powerful and knows all; therefore their word is like gospel. This idea was prominent in Elizabethan England, with Queen Elizabeth I's authority accepted above all else. This is why Claudius, the King of Denmark, can get away with a lot, even if he is deceptive. The lack of trust in *Hamlet* also reflects the lack of trust in Shakespeare's time; political instability was widespread due to the imminent transfer of power to King James I, as well as religious rifts between Catholics and Protestants.

Based on this doctrine, Claudius was able to manipulate many characters into conducting surveillance on his behalf. However, their **morally unscrupulous behaviour leads to their downfall.** For example, Rosencrantz and Guildenstern, Hamlet's friends, were commissioned by the King to spy on Hamlet and find out why he went mad, thus breaking the trust of Hamlet, and in the end, Hamlet betrayed them by signing their death warrant. Similarly, Laertes' revenge plot was greatly inspired by the words of Claudius, though backfired and resulted in his death. Once again, Horatio is the only one who does not engage in such duplicitous behaviour, and is rewarded with Hamlet's continuous trust.

Unscrupulous: corrupt or without moral principles like honesty.

Action and inaction

The theme of action and inaction throughout Hamlet is very prevalent, and has many complex origins. In medieval dramas about morality, before Shakespeare's time, a common theatrical device was called **psychomania** – that is, an angel on one shoulder and a devil on the other. It was a great visual story telling method to demonstrate an individual's internal conflict externally. However, Shakespeare innovates this device by internalising this conflict within Hamlet's mind, and in doing so helps to present the human experience to audiences with great clarity. This is why he **constantly contemplates the complexities of life, and whether or not he should avenge his father in a morally corrupt manner.** This leads to Hamlet's repeated procrastination and inaction; it is in his nature to be conflicted about his actions, which causes a delay. Although, as expressed by Laertes, this should not be something that Hamlet is ashamed about; "Nature her custom holds / Let shame say what it will." In fact, it makes him human.

This theme is central in the creation of character foils within *Hamlet*. Most prominently, Hamlet's inaction juxtaposes the impulsive actions of Laertes and Fortinbras. Where Hamlet constantly finds ways to put off his revenge, both Laertes and Fortinbras immediately take action. They are not as conflicted about the complexities of life, and are more driven by their perceived obligations.

Hamlet is also trying to deal with the possible guilt of murder, which further compounds his inaction, and can be partially attributed to Freud's notion of the Oedipus Complex. This idea stems from psychoanalysis, though has been used to interpret the actions of literary characters. For instance, Ernst Jones did this in his studies from 1949, identifying that Hamlet's regular "paralysis of doubt" only arises "in the matter of revenge", making him a "pseudo-procrastinator").

Alternative readings: ways of analysing texts that challenge the typical beliefs and values of a society. New philosophical or political perspectives can be applied to the plot and character behaviours.

His inadequate repression of his desire for maternal possession, as well as his subjective Renaissance Humanist tendencies, forces an emotional alignment to Claudius as his mother's new spouse that prevents Hamlet from acting out in clear conscience.

Adding **alternative readings** such as this one into your essays also helps to demonstrate the enduring form of *Hamlet*, and can help add complexity to your contention. Conducting research on other alternative readings can also allow you to strengthen your own opinions and ideas regarding the play. But, don't forget, **the most important 'reading' to include is your own**. You have to trust your own perspective and demonstrate that to the markers by providing plenty of supporting analysis.

As you can probably tell from reading about these key themes, they all work together to add meaning to *Hamlet*. They have been interwoven by Shakespeare, and should be understood holistically to get the most meaning out of the text. The ideas occur as motifs, and can help you to divide your essay and analysis up cohesively.

Section 6
Structural Features Analysis

The structural features of *Hamlet* should make up a large portion of your analysis, so it's important that you are aware of the techniques and devices utilised by Shakespeare to create meaning. While it is good to include techniques like similes, personification, and imagery, looking beyond that is where you are going to find the top marks. Try to extend your analysis to be more customised to the text type. For example, if you were analysing a film holistically, you would look at camera angles, shots, lighting, and music, amongst other things. Similarly, if you were analysing a poem, it would be important to look at rhyming patterns and extended metaphors. Therefore, you have to look for the same specifics when analysing plays and dramas, because it is a unique storytelling genre. We are going to analyse all of these structural features in this section.

Acts and scenes

Acts and scenes are the key forms of structure in plays in a typical sense, with the purpose of dividing the play into different stages of action. The whole play is divided into five linear acts, each with scenes of contrasting tension and audience interest. The story is as follows:

- **Act 1: Exposition** – this includes bringing the audience up to speed with what's happening in the play, or describing the setting, among other things.
- **Act 2: Conflict** – a problem has arisen and is causing tension among characters.
- **Act 3: Crisis** – something really bad happens and changes the tone of the play.
- **Act 4: Counter Stroke** – some more bad things happen, building tension and suspense for audience members.
- **Act 5: Catastrophe** – typical of many Shakespearean tragedies at this point, this is usually where all the main characters die.

The scenes also play a role in maintaining interest and creating contrast. By varying length, subject matter, or even which characters are involved in the scene, audiences stay engaged with the plot. However once again, for this contrast to be meaningful, there have to be some **parallels between scenes** as well. This is often achieved by **characterisation.** Significantly, character foils encourages audiences to compare the actions of major characters. We can follow the actions of Hamlet, Laertes, and Fortinbras, just as an example, and see how they deal with similar issues in different ways across all five acts.

Staging and stage directions

Shakespeare famously did not offer his actors many stage directions. Costumes and props were both pretty minimal, and **actors were often asked to present a representation of events on stage and demonstrate the meaning, rather than seek realism.** Additionally, it is important to consider the time frame in which Shakespeare's plays were performed. *Hamlet* obviously does not take place in real time. Instead, the scene and/or stage are manipulated to emulate the idea of time. For example, Act 1 Scene 1 is supposed to go from midnight to dawn, but this is not possible. Instead, it only takes a matter of fifteen minutes on stage. In a metatheatrical sense, **this time elasticity reminds the audience that they are watching a play and not observing real life.**

Character foils

Character foils are a very prominent feature in *Hamlet*, used by Shakespeare to develop characters and **highlight behaviours or flaws.** Essentially, character foils provide two or more contrasting characters, typically the protagonist and some other major character(s). However, for these different behaviours to be obvious, the characters first have to have some things in common. For a clear example, consider Hamlet and Laertes. While **Hamlet struggles with delay and contemplation** for the entire play, **Laertes always wants to spring into action immediately.** Their behaviours stand in stark contrast to one another, yet they are linked by their **filial obligations to their murdered fathers.**

In terms of character types, it is also important to address **archetypes** throughout *Hamlet*. Loosely based on some stereotypes, Hamlet can be classed as somewhat of an **anti-hero** (though the lines are blurred). His character foil, Laertes, acts as a **shadow.** Some typical conflicts are also demonstrated, such as that between Hamlet and his father. Ophelia also represents a pretty popular character archetype: the damsel in distress.

Hamlet's soliloquies

Soliloquies and their function

Soliloquies allow characters in a play to speak their thoughts aloud when they are alone, and serve several purposes in Shakespeare's *Hamlet*. By engaging in an act of **self-communion** (talking to oneself) via a soliloquy, characters are able to address the audience without the knowledge of other characters. It may give characters a chance to persuade the audience to be on their side by giving their side of events, or allow characters to come to terms with their own feelings. It also allows **direct access to the character's innermost thoughts and exposes their real character** via a more truthful expression of emotions. In this entire play, Hamlet performs a total of seven soliloquies, each with their unique tone and function.

Act 1 Scene 2

This first soliloquy addresses Hamlet's **suicidal thoughts** due his father's death and his mother's hasty remarriage to Claudius. He is **disillusioned with life, and projects his anger toward women,** since he feels that Gertrude has betrayed him. There is a common theme of corruption as seen through, "O that this too too sullied flesh would melt, / Thaw, and resolve itself into a dew!" (In various editions, "sullied" has been substituted for "solid" or "sallied," but they essentially mean the same thing!) Other negative nature imagery is used, with Hamlet calling Denmark an "unweeded garden" due to its imminent corruption. Hamlet also expresses **melancholy** relating to the father and the world that he feels he has lost through this **elegy.**

Hamlet further **condemns his mother for the lack of delay in her decision to marry Claudius,** her ex-brother-in-law, and getting into "incestuous sheets." He makes many **allusions to God and sin** as well, particularly relating Gertrude's action to Eve's sin in a misogynistic tone. Overall, we get the sense that **Hamlet has a lot of passion,** which makes him **exaggerate** the facts. His reference to the Sixth Commandment – thou shalt not kill – also highlights his fascination with the afterlife and spirituality. Finally, it's useful to recognise that **Hamlet juxtaposes a lot of virtues and ideas,** such as **Hyperion and satyr**, or heaven and earth.

Melancholy: a deep, pensive sadness or depression.

Elegy: a verse of serious reflection about death.

Hyperion and satyr: a Greek myth used by Hamlet to glorify his father as the god-like figure of Hyperion whilst degrading Claudius as a grotesque half-man half-goat satyr, symbolic of sexual corruption.

Act 1 Scene 5

Following the Ghost's declaration that he was murdered, **Hamlet enters a state of confusion and distress.** He has become fervent, and does not know if he should take immediate action and avenge his father. This impassion is conveyed through his **frequently fragmented speech filled with tautology.** He also uses short phrases and rhetorical questions to emulate his confusion. This can be seen in the quote, "O all you host of heaven! O earth! what else? / And shall I couple hell? O, fie! — Hold, my heart." In these opening lines of the soliloquy, we can already see his **bewilderment.** Through another religious allusion, he is addressing everyone that he can think of; people in heaven, hell, and earth. This inner conflict about avenging his father stems from his **filial obligation and his disgust toward Gertrude and Claudius' actions.**

Tautology: an unnecessary repetition of a particular idea.

Act 2 Scene 2

This is a **transformative** soliloquy in which Hamlet visibly **decides between his previous passionate self-loathing, and an attempt of following through with reason.** This particularly applies to his moral dilemma of avenging his father. He is testing his father's word and Claudius' conscience, by introducing the play-within-a-play. Hamlet's initial speech imitates that of Pyrrhus from the play, again with short phrases and insults. His first line encapsulates this: "Ay, so, God b' wi' ye! / Now I am alone. / O, what a rogue and peasant slave am I!" Hamlet's repetition of "villain" also reflects his rage and the way in which he is trying to work through his thoughts and feelings. However, **Hamlet transitions into a new state of mind as the soliloquy progresses. He is determined to follow reason and not rely on destiny,** as demonstrated through his smoother, more regular rhythm of speech.

Act 3 Scene 1

One of the most popular lines in English literature comes from this soliloquy: "To be, or not to be: that is the question." By this point in the play, Hamlet has experienced even more betrayal and as such contemplates suicide even more frequently. The aforementioned famous phrase **implies life or death** in a direct sense. Though, Hamlet never directly talks about himself in this scenario, and instead chooses to use plural pronouns like "we." This suggests that Hamlet is posing a more philosophical debate between the abstract concepts of life and death.

Further, Hamlet is also asking **if it is worth living unhappily at all.** He is unsure if putting up with life's burdens is actually worth it. Once again, Hamlet is greatly conflicted because he doesn't know whether or not to take action. C.S. Lewis (famed author of the *Chronicles of Narnia*) believes that this is **not a result of Hamlet's fear of death, but rather a fear of life after death and the unknown.**

This delay also transfers into his revenge plot towards Claudius. He is still **unsure whether to be passive and thoughtful, or take immediate action.** Something important to recognise with this soliloquy, and a couple of others, is that **they aren't performed in complete isolation.** For example, Claudius and Polonius are hanging around within earshot while Hamlet performs this soliloquy, thus subtly reminding audiences about the pervasive surveillance throughout the play.

Act 3 Scene 2

This soliloquy demonstrates Hamlet's supposed **readiness to take action against Claudius.** He is using typical language of vengeance to try and create the image that he is a villain: "Tis now the very witching time of night, / When churchyards yawn, and hell itself breathes out / Contagion to this world." Although, his performance doesn't seem all that convincing (it is almost as though he is trying to trick himself into believing his own words), this nevertheless creates tension for the audience, as it is unclear how Hamlet is going to act in the ensuing scenes. The second half of the soliloquy is concerned with Gertrude. Hamlet wishes to avoid being violent against her, as per his father's orders, and because he is concerned for her soul. He says, "I will speak daggers to her, but use none," which does actually contradict his earlier statements. Now, he doesn't want to follow through with "unnatural" murderous actions, though, his impressionable personality means that he was greatly influenced by *The Mousetrap*. This facilitated his cold-blooded murder of Polonius in Act 3 Scene 4, but made him "weep" afterwards.

Act 3 Scene 3

The sixth soliloquy **takes place after Hamlet concludes that Claudius is guilty of murder** because of his reaction to *The Mousetrap*. However, he decides that he won't do it immediately, for if Hamlet kills Claudius while he is praying, Claudius will be forgiven by God for his sins and sent to heaven. Hamlet thinks that this is unjust, since he believes Claudius sent Old Hamlet to purgatory. Hence, Hamlet decides in this soliloquy that he will delay his action even further. The single word "No." in line 87 is probably the most assured Hamlet is in his decisions for the whole play.

Act 4 Scene 4

In Hamlet's final soliloquy of the play, he is still **inquisitive about the nature of man and his honour, as well as the reason as to why he has delayed the revenge plot so long.** "How all occasions do inform against me / And spur my dull revenge!" Once again, Hamlet is not really alone when performing this soliloquy, as Rosencrantz and Guildenstern are spying on him. Hamlet tries to inspire himself into action once again, but a **paradox** is created. Hamlet is confused as to why Fortinbras, someone whom he has admired in the past, is going to such lengths to gain so little. He cannot comprehend the point, because he sees no honour in it, even though he himself is on a quest of honour for his father. So, here's the paradox: **Hamlet has admired Fortinbras for his action, while simultaneously condemning him for his absurd actions and futile quest for honour.** It's clear that **Hamlet is frustrated with himself** because of this, due to his speech: 26 monosyllabic words are used in lines 43 to 46, almost as a **powerful imitation of his own short emotional fuse.**

Paradox: a statement which cannot necessarily be solved using sound reasoning, as it leads to logically unacceptable or contradictory conclusions.

Metatheatre

Metatheatre **draws attention towards the fictitious nature of plays, and challenges the play's ability to present reality, since it seems conscious that it is not real life.** Shakespeare frequently draws attention to the fact that the audience is watching a play, often by utilising anti-illusionist devices such as soliloquies, asides, and the play-within-a-play called *The Mousetrap*. Since the events in that play actually reflect the events in Shakespeare's play, it creates another **metatheatrical layer; it makes audiences aware that they are watching a play.** This is also called a **frame narrative**; for example, *The Mousetrap* mirrors Hamlet's inaction and delay, and contains the same **motifs of reflections, doubles, and mirroring** as Shakespeare's *Hamlet*. We see reflections in characters via their character foils, like Hamlet, Laertes, Fortinbras and even Ophelia, and we also observe many instances of word plays with double meaning. However, the incredibly skilful thing about Shakespeare's play is that even though audiences are made aware of the fact that they're watching a play, **they still remain engaged with the plot and can sympathise with the multidimensional characters.**

> **Frame narrative:** a story-within-a-story that echoes the main thematic searches
>
> **Motif:** a dominant, recurring idea throughout a text or artwork.

Intertextuality

Throughout *Hamlet*, Shakespeare alludes to many significant events, texts, and people in order to shape his own text while communicating universal ideas. Most prominently, Shakespeare makes many **allusions to the Bible and Christianity.** For instance, according to the Bible, the character of Cain became the first murderer after he killed his own brother in Genesis 4:10-12, which can be said to add depth to Claudius' **fratricidal** troubles. In the same vein, the gravediggers are often read as allusions to **Adam and Eve,** as they believe that their work is in keeping with Adam's profession of digging with his own arms. By providing this intertextual reference to the Bible, **Shakespeare gives the two gravediggers a clear sense of life's purpose.**

> **Fratricide:** killing one's brother or sister.

There are also several allusions to historical events and figures which contextualise the actions of the characters in *Hamlet*. When Hamlet comes across Yorick's skull, he tries to personify it and give it a voice. Initially, he generalises its character; it could be a court jester, or a nobleman. However, once he proposes that it could be Alexander the Great or even Julius Caesar, who were great historical figures but may now by mere dust, **a more personal connection is developed between the events in Hamlet and the events of real life. Through this, Shakespeare reinforces the notion that no matter who you are, we all end up in the same place, eaten by the same worms.**

Language and literary devices

By now, you should be very familiar with a multitude of language techniques and literary devices, and be able to pick them out as you read though texts. The list below is not exhaustive, but will give you an idea of what to look out for and how to include it in your essays.

Language

In many of his plays, Shakespeare uses **variations in verse and prose to distinguish between character's social ranks and their states of mind.** Where verse tends to have a regular rhythm and kind of imitates poetry with an **iambic pentameter,** prose is closer to our normal language and cadence of speech. For example, the labouring gravediggers, who are part of one of the lowest classes in the social hierarchy, speak in prose. Contrastingly, Claudius as the monarch always speaks in verse, with his speech informed by the code of society – that is, the Divine Right of Kings.

Hamlet's speech is very peculiar. **His register changes to coincide with his tragic progression and transition into action.** He initially speaks in verse because he is part of the royal family. However, he speaks in prose while he acts mad and when he ultimately descends into madness by the final scene.

Many of the phrases used in Hamlet are specially crafted to convey multiple layers of meaning. Many comments, especially those made by Hamlet, have dual meanings, ultimately highlighting Hamlet's wit and intelligence. This makes it all the more reasonable that he would contemplate murder for so long; he does not want to corrupt his morals. His **frequent negation** in phrases like "nay," "not so much," and "not too," also demonstrates his internal anguish.

Iambic pentameter: an iamb is an unaccented syllable followed by an accented one. Therefore, an iambic pentameter is made up of five of these measures, which makes each line ten syllables.

Negation: the denial of something.

Irony and humour

Irony is a literary technique that **allows the audience to recognise the full significance of a character's words or actions, even when this is unknown to the character.** This is often used to infuse humour into the drama and appeal to the crowd, particularly the commoners. There are several forms of irony that are present in *Hamlet* in order to provide this comic relief. **Dramatic irony** is very prominent in plays, as it involves **sharing information with the audience that other characters are unaware of.** This can be seen in Hamlet's feigned madness, which he and Horatio know about, but leaves other characters at a loss in explaining Hamlet's actions. By contrast, **situational irony is humour in an event that occurs.** In the case of *Hamlet*, this is epitomised by Laertes switching swords with Hamlet and his backfired revenge plot, causing a catastrophic regicide. Additionally, **verbal irony goes hand in hand with word play, as it involves ironic humour in dialogue.** This is seen in Hamlet's world play through, "A little more than kin, and less than kind," as explained on page 10. Humour also comes in different forms beyond irony. Many individual characters are portrayed with humorous dialogue in order to provide some contrast and lighten the mood. For example, Osric's babbling and Hamlet's mockery is intended to be humorous, as are the puns made by the gravediggers.

Repetition

Epizeuxis: the repetition of a single word or phrase in quick succession.

Repetition is frequently used for **emphasis,** but also to **demonstrate the characters' descent into madness.** In many instances, Hamlet himself repeats his words; in fact, when he first feigns madness, he utilises **epizeuxis** and says, "words, words, words." Later, when Hamlet redirects his madness towards Gertrude because of her betrayal, he repeats that she is "A rat! A rat!" Additionally, there is a significant amount of repetition in Ophelia's sing-song madness, further emphasising the **emotionally regressive** nature of her behaviour.

Regressive: returning to a less developed (or in this case, more child-like) state.

Symbolism

Symbolism is great to include in your analysis, because most of the time you will be able to extract much deeper meaning than you otherwise would with just a surface-level incorporation of quotes. You can connect symbols to larger motifs, extended metaphors, or link them to the subjective framework of the author. There is plenty of symbolism to be found in *Hamlet* – one of the most obvious examples of which are Ophelia's flowers. Flowers alone symbolise Ophelia's fragile beauty and innocence. However, Shakespeare takes it one step further and uses individual types of flowers to send important messages to characters and audiences, especially once she goes mad. The following is a list of some flowers she gifts in Act 4 Scene 5 at the height of her madness.

- **Rosemary and pansies:** for **Laertes,** symbolising **remembrance and thoughts.**
- **Fennel and columbine:** for **Claudius,** as an accusation of **adultery and unfaithfulness.**
- **Rue:** for **Gertrude,** a symbol of **bitterness** and **adultery. Ophelia also keeps some rue for herself.**
- **Daisy:** a symbol of **innocence** and **tenderness,** which **she does not gift to anyone,** as she does not believe that there is any faith left for the corrupt Danish court.
- **Violets:** she reserves these for her dead father **Polonius,** as they symbolise **faithfulness** and **loyalty.** Violets also look as though their heads are hanging in grief, which is an interesting connection to Polonius' murder.

Imagery

Imagery **allows audiences to engage with the play beyond the words and literal meanings.** Much of the imagery in *Hamlet* allows for **cohesion** across the play, and two of the most prominent examples of this are the **ear/ hearing imagery** and **disease/ corruption imagery.**

The motifs of ears and hearing spans across the whole play. The ghost of Old Hamlet claims Claudius poured a "leperous distilment" of poison into his ear. This physical action of dropping poison into Old Hamlet's ear is a representation of the betrayal Claudius commits against him. However, as expressed by dialogue, **words can function as poison to the ear as well and lead to corruption.** Old Hamlet claims that, by lying about the murder, Claudius has poisoned "the whole ear of Denmark" and "rankly abused" it. Hamlet then furthers this motif when writing his letter to Horatio, stating "I have words to speak in thine ear that will make thee numb."

These examples link nicely with another prominent notion in Hamlet: disease/ corruption imagery. In the first act, Marcellus acknowledges "something is rotten" in Denmark, foreshadowing the ensuing corruption. Many of the characters remark upon their own varying state of disease or illness: Hamlet says, "my wit's diseased," and Laertes discusses the "very sickness in [his] heart" following his family tragedies. Ophelia's madness is also credited as the "poison of deep grief." **These characters are grieving the corruption of Denmark and internalising the issues. The problems of the state are tainting everyone's state of mind.** As Hamlet dies, acting as the agent of his own redemption from moral corruption, he in some ways 'cures' Denmark by extension. However, it is the powerful, headstrong, and responsible Fortinbras that ultimately provides hope for the future of the kingdom.

Section 7

Quote Bank

Revenge, action, and inaction

Quote	Character	Act/Scene
"Sulfurous and tormenting flames [of purgatory]"	The Ghost	Act 1 Scene 5
"Foul, strange and unnatural [murder]"	The Ghost	Act 1 Scene 5
"I'll have these players / Play something like the murder of my father / Before mine uncle. I'll observe his looks."	Hamlet	Act 2 Scene 2
"The play's the thing/ Wherein I'll catch the conscience of the king."	Hamlet	Act 2 Scene 2
"Purpose is but the slave to memory, / Of violent birth, but poor validity."	Player King	Act 3 Scene 2
"What to ourselves in passion we propose, / The passion ending, doth the purpose lose."	Player King	Act 3 Scene 2
"Let the galled jade wince, our withers are unwrung."	Hamlet	Act 3 Scene 2
"I will speak daggers to her, but use none."	Hamlet	Act 3 Scene 2
"Oh, what a rash and bloody deed this is!"	Gertrude	Act 3 Scene 4
"Thou find'st to be too busy is some danger."	Hamlet	Act 3 Scene 4
"Oh, from this time forth, / My thoughts be bloody, or be nothing worth!"	Hamlet	Act 3 Scene 4
"How all occasions do inform against me / And spur my dull revenge!"	Hamlet	Act 3 Scene 7
"Revenge should have no bounds."	Laertes	Act 3 Scene 3
"To cut his throat i' th' church."	Laertes	Act 3 Scene 7
"Nature her custom holds / Let shame say what it will."	Polonius	Act 5 Scene 1
"Their defeat does by their own insinuation grow."	Hamlet	Act 5 Scene 2

Appearance and reality

"Though yet of Hamlet our late brother's death / The memory be green."	Claudius	Act 1 Scene 2
"A little more than kin and less than kind."	Hamlet	Act 1 Scene 2
"Not so, my lord. I am too much i' the sun."	Hamlet	Act 1 Scene 2
"This above all: To thine own self be true."	Polonius	Act 1 Scene 3
Hamlet's "antic disposition"	Hamlet	Act 1 Scene 5
"Words, words, words" and "except my life, except my life, except my life"	Hamlet	Act 2 Scene 2
"Though this be madness, yet there is method in't"	Hamlet	Act 2 Scene 2
"I am but mad north-north-west. When the wind is southerly, I know a hawk from a handsaw"	Hamlet	Act 2 Scene 2
"to hold as 'twere the mirror up to nature"	Hamlet	Act 3 Scene 2
"One scene of [the play] comes near the circumstance / Which I have told thee of my father's death"	Hamlet	Act 3 Scene 2
"Mad as the sea and wind when both contend / Which is the mightier"	Ophelia	Act 4 Scene 1
"If Hamlet from himself be ta'en away, / And when he's not himself does wrong Laertes, / Then Hamlet does it not. Hamlet denies it. / Who does it, then? His madness."	Hamlet	Act 5 Scene 2

Mortality, humanity, and fate

"All that lives must die"	Gertrude	Act 1 Scene 2
"What a piece of work is a man! How noble in reason, how infinite in faculty, in form and moving how express and admirable, in action how like an angel, in apprehension how like a god."	Hamlet	Act 2 Scene 2
"There is nothing either good or bad, but thinking makes it so"	Hamlet	Act 2 Scene 2
"And yet, to me, what is this quintessence of dust? Man delights not me"	Hamlet	Act 2 Scene 2
"To be or not to be: that is the question..."	Hamlet	Act 3 Scene 1
"For who would bear the whips and scorn of time, / Th' oppressor's wrong... When he himself might his quietus make/With a bare bodkin?"	Hamlet	Act 3 Scene 1
"Makes us rather bear those ills we have"	Hamlet	Act 3 Scene 2
"Some necessary question of the play be then to be considered"	Hamlet	Act 3 Scene 2
"Sir, I lack advancement"	Hamlet	Act 3 Scene 3
"The conscience does make cowards of us all"	Hamlet	Act 3 Scene 3
"I must be cruel only to be kind"	Hamlet	Act 3 Scene 4
"What is a man, if his chief good and market of his time be but to sleep and feed?"	Hamlet	Act 4 Scene 4
"When sorrows come, they come not single spies. But in battalions!"	Claudius	Act 4 Scene 5
"That skull had a tongue in it and could sing once"	Hamlet	Act 5 Scene 1
"A man's life no more than to say 'one'"	Hamlet	Act 5 Scene 2

Religion

"O all you host of heaven! O earth! What else?/ And shall I couple hell? O, fie! — Hold, my heart..."	Hamlet	Act 1 Scene 5
"Then is doomsday near."	Hamlet	Act 2 Scene 1
"'Tis too much proved, that with devotion's visage / And pious action we do sugar o'er / The devil himself."	Polonius	Act 3 Scene 1
'Tis now the very witching time of night,/ When churchyards yawn, and hell itself breathes out / Contagion to this world..."	Hamlet	Act 3 Scene 2
"Try what repentance can."	Claudius	Act 3 Scene 3

Women and sex

"incestuous sheets"	Hamlet	Act 1 Scene 2
"This is the very ecstasy of love, / Whose violent property leads itself / And leads the will to desperate undertakings"	Polonius	Act 2 Scene 1
"I have a daughter – have while she is mine"	Polonius	Act 2 Scene 2
"I shall obey you."	Gertrude	Act 3 Scene 1
"Get thee to a nunnery!"	Hamlet	Act 3 Scene 1
"The lady doth protest too much, methinks."	Gertrude	Act 3 Scene 2
"How now, a rat?"	Hamlet	Act 3 Scene 4
"Nay, but to live/ In the rank sweat of an enseaméd med, / Stewed in corruption, honeying and making love / Over the nasty sty"	Hamlet	Act 3 Scene 4

Surveillance and trust

Quote	Character	Location
"Who's there?"	Barnardo	Act 1 Scene 1
"Listen to many, speak to a few."	Polonius	Act 1 Scene 3
"Observe his inclination in yourself."	Polonius	Act 2 Scene 1
"I entreat you both / That, being of so young days brought up with him / And since so neighboured to his youth and 'havior, / That you vouchsafe your rest here in our court / Some little time so by your companies / To draw him on to pleasures and to gather…"	Claudius	Act 3 Scene 1
"Madness in great ones must not unwatched go."	Claudius	Act 3 Scene 1
"I prithee, when thou seest that act afoot /… Observe mine uncle…"	Hamlet	Act 3 Scene 2
"Now might I do it pat. Now he is a-praying. / And now I'll do it. And so he goes to heaven. / And so am I revenged…"	Hamlet	Act 3 Scene 3

Imagery

Quote	Character	Location
"'Tis bitter cold, and I am sick at heart."	Francisco	Act 1 Scene 1
"Sit down awhile/ And let us once again assail your ears"	Barnardo	Act 1 Scene 1
"This bodes some strange eruption to our state."	Horatio	Act 1 Scene 1
"O that this too too sullied flesh would melt, / Thaw, and resolve itself into a dew!"	Hamlet	Act 1 Scene 2
"Something is rotten in the state of Denmark."	Marcellus	Act 1 Scene 4
"The leprous distilment, whose effect / Holds such an enmity with blood of man"	The Ghost	Act 1 Scene 5
"Poisons him i' th' garden for 's estate."	Hamlet	Act 3 Scene 2
"Like the owner of a foul disease, / To keep it from divulging, let it feed / Even on the pith of life."	Claudius	Act 4 Scene 1
"Lay her i' th' earth, / And from her fair and unpolluted flesh/ May violets spring!"	Laertes	Act 5 Scene 1

Section 8

Sample Essays

Essay One

QUESTION: Discuss the ways in which Shakespeare's *Hamlet* explores uncomfortable truths.

ESSAY	COMMENTS
INTRODUCTION William Shakespeare's Senecan revenge tragedy, *Hamlet*, presents to its audience a confronting exploration of the disparities of a decaying world.[3] Though shaped by Shakespeare's socio-political Elizabethan context, *Hamlet* has been appreciated across centuries due to its compassionate evaluation of uncomfortable truths[2] in human behaviour, misogyny, the inquisitive human temperament, and the meaning of life itself. These universally engaging elements have been re-interpreted by critics and audiences over several centuries, since "reality is in the reader's mind" (W. Hazlitt, 1817),[3] thus ultimately facilitating the textual integrity of *Hamlet*.	1. Note this quick summary of the play. This is all you really need to address in terms of the play's content, rather than retelling the whole story. You can add some more plot context as you analyse the play in your body paragraphs. 2. It is important to use the key words of the prompt in your introduction to ensure your marker can see the overt relevance of your essay (as well as the more covert links you make to the ideas in the prompt). 3. Though not always required, incorporating academic quotes can help to enhance your argument (provided you don't let them do all the talking for you).

PARAGRAPH 1

Human curiousity is a universal trait that is, though in Shakespeare's *Hamlet,* it is shown to unearth various inconvenient truths.[4] The metatheatrical nature of *Hamlet* allows for the immediate investigation into such behaviour, as the play begins in medias res.[5] This contrived chaos is exacerbated with Bernardo's rhetorical dialogue, "Who's there?", which cleverly foreshadows the motivic diseased disorder within the "rotten... state of Denmark." Hamlet's first soliloquy further[6] exposes his innermost thoughts, while presenting an insight into his physical **synecdochical**[7] "sallied flesh" with which audiences can empathise. His frequent negation – "nay, not so much, not two" – demonstrates his internal anguish; uncertainty is attached to his father's death and his widowed mother's hasty conjugation, leading to Hamlet's uncomfortable discovery regarding the fallibility of human memory. The difficulty of determining truth within an ambiguous society is carefully constructed within all of Hamlet's soliloquies,[8] with "some sublime passages... of the greatest genius." (Voltaire, 1748)[9] Thus, the integral characters of Hamlet create a meta-fictional dimension that allows audiences to appreciate the value of humanity empathetically.

4. This topic sentence attacks the question, while conveying to the marker that we intend to explore a key theme of the play in this paragraph.
5. Seamless use of metalanguage helps show your assessor that you can write fluently about the text's structural features.
6. Note how this paragraph has already smoothly transitioned between quotes and analysis? This is typical of high-range pieces, so emulating this in your own work is almost guaranteed to improve your marks!
7. **Synecdoche:** a figure of speech in which one part of a whole is used to represent the entire concept.
8. This short reference to the dramatic structure helps to broaden the type of analysis, beyond language techniques.
9. Adding a couple of critical quotes in your essay can be useful, but make sure that you are maintaining your own opinion above all else.

PARAGRAPH 2

Furthermore, the raw volatility of human emotion in *Hamlet* has been reinterpreted to suit alternative readings, which expose somewhat uncomfortable truths. For instance, the **duality**[10] of appearance and reality is enhanced through the motif of ears and imagery of the "leperous distilment" in the "porches of [King Hamlet's] ear," symbolising Claudius' powerful words poisoning King Hamlet's mind and instigating Hamlet's corruption. This quote performed as part of a monologue allows audiences to empathise with the characters, in particular Hamlet, and there are several hints to his emotional state that compound our sympathy for him. Hamlet's delay of Claudius' murder, for one, can be read through the lens of an Oedipus Complex, accentuated by the mise-en-abyme[11] of *The Mousetrap*. However, Ernest Jones posed that Hamlet's regularly identified "paralysis of doubt" only arises "in the matter of revenge", making him a "pseudo-procrastinator" (1949)[12]. His inadequate repression of his desire for maternal possession, as well as his subjective Renaissance Humanist tendencies[13], forces an emotional alignment to Claudius as his mother's new spouse that prevents Hamlet from acting out in clear conscience. Laurence Olivier's 1948 intensely incestuous enactment[13] promotes this uncomfortable version of truth, which heavily sexualises Hamlet and Gertrude's complex filial relationship, further highlighting the integral enduring form of *Hamlet*. This Freudian analysis is pivotal in Hamlet's argument with his mother, with the juxtaposed virtues of his dead "Hyperion," with the reigning regicidal "satyr." Hence, the essence of human guilt

10. **Duality:** dividing a singular concept into two contrasting ideas.
11. **Mise-en-abyme:** placing a copy of an image or text within itself, giving the illusion of an infinitely recurring sequence.
12. Reference to literary theory and analysis.
13. There are several links to context in this paragraph, which demonstrates thorough research.
14. Including new interpretations of *Hamlet* highlights its integrity.

has been represented and appreciated by different audiences, since "there are more Hamlets than actors to play them." (H. Bloom, 1998) – modern individuals are able to continually reinterpret and empathise with Hamlet's delay as his **hamartia**.[15]

PARAGRAPH 3

The misogyny perpetuated throughout *Hamlet* highlights a rigid, socially pre-scribed relationship between Elizabethan males and females and as such exposes an uncomfortable societal truth. Shakespeare's social hierarchy indicated an intense **patriarchal paternalism**;[15] in particular, Ophelia epitomizes the archetypal womanly values of silence, chastity, and obedience, and thus "suffers a series of patriarchal oppressions" (E. Hamana, 1988), reflecting the empathetic perspective of second-wave feminism. This is juxtaposed by Hamlet's perception of moral corruption and female subordination, manifested through the extended metaphor, "frailty thy name is woman" and the repetitive **dysphemism**[16] of Gertrude as "A rat! A rat!" Hence, through *Hamlet*, Shakespeare depicts women as being the biblical root of all corruption; Gertrude is symbolic of Eve in devising contracts with the Devil to obtain a higher status in society, and Hamlet commanding Ophelia to "get thee to a nunnery" dualistically presents him as wanting to protect her from moral corruption whilst also degrading her sexually. A modern feminist reading emphasises Ophelia's helpless and eventual "mad" disposition – depicted through her fluctuation between prose and verse[17] in Act 4 – as a result of Hamlet's distrust of women. Thus, *Hamlet* enables various audiences to understand the harsh truths of human rhythms and relationships.

15. **Hamartia:** a fatal flaw in character that leads to the downfall of a tragic hero/heroine.

15. **Patriarchal paternalism:** a society in which a male-controlled government or organisation limits a particular minority's liberty and autonomy (specifically women).
16. **Dysphemism**: a derogatory term with negative connotations.
17. Once again, this analysis of the structural and dramatic features of Hamlet goes beyond the typical metaphor/symbolism/simile/personification analysis. It develops the sophistication of your writing.

PARAGRAPH 4

Hamlet's existential anxieties ultimately exacerbate human isolation and the power of the mind as a sanctuary of thought. Shakespeare's representation of these ideas through literature allows audiences to connect and empathise with life's unpleasant actualities. The fourth soliloquy depicts Hamlet's continuous pondering within his mind – "to be, or not to be" – alluding to the fundamental question of life and death. Such ramifications of mortality are reflected to the audience through collective pronouns, "and makes us rather bear those ills we have." Furthermore, an even greater understanding of human existence is reached in the graveyard where Hamlet contemplates Yorick's personified skull and alludes to Alexander the Great, who "returneth into dust." In doing so, Hamlet **cathartically**[18] confronts the symbolic face of death, and his emotional façade is lifted to expose his foreshadowed "antic disposition." Once Hamlet finds the purpose of individual fulfilment, – "What is a man / if his chief good and market of his time / be but to sleep and feed?" – his ensuing actions demonstrate an unfortunate abandonment of self-identity; the employment of third person narrative is a bizarre subversion of a character previously obsessed with "I".[19] Therefore, the play's deep exploration into human mortality is critical factor in allowing audiences to appreciate *Hamlet* with empathy.

18. **Catharsis**: releasing strong or repressed emotions, which ultimately provides relief

19. These sentences have examined three or four small but significant techniques (symbolism, foreshadowing, pronouns) which together form a holistic analysis of Hamlet's trajectory towards the end of the play.

CONCLUSION

Ultimately[20], the abstruse definition of human nature allows Shakespeare's *Hamlet* to be appreciated in distinctive ways across differing **zeitgeists.**[21] That the protagonists have such tragic self-awareness of this uncertainty makes *Hamlet* an alluring play that has allowed us as modern responders to draw our own conclusions of eternal uncomfortable truths. Shakespeare's challenging but invaluable reflection of humanity as a victim of the chaos of its world, unable to attain any certainty of its experiences, facilities the contemporary extraction of individual meaning, because after all, "It is we who are Hamlet" (Hazlitt, 1817).[22]

20. The conclusion should serve a few purposes: summarise your arguments, reiterate your contention, and leave a final good impression on your marker.

21. **Zeitgeist:** the defining mood of a particular historical period, shaped by the prominent ideas and beliefs.

22. As with all critical quotes, don't let them do all of the work for you. It can often be better to avoid ever ending a paragraph with a quote (from the text or otherwise) as this at least forces you to put your final point in your own words, but provided your paragraph has made its thesis clear, a quote can be a nice, resonant way to conclude.

Essay Two

QUESTION: The world of Shakespeare's *Hamlet* is portrayed as disturbed and imbalanced. To what extent do you agree?

ESSAY	COMMENTS
INTRODUCTION Central to coherent and enduring literature is its ability to reflect the harsh realities of the world and provide a portrait of natural imbalances.[1] This is expressed through William Shakespeare's revenge tragedy, *Hamlet*, which candidly explores how relationships in this imbalanced world can be unworthy, malicious, at times pitiful, and destined to fail. By drawing on this, Shakespeare paints a bleak portrait of a world filled with disturbing revenge, madness, and gender inequalities[2] that has transcended audiences across cultures and centuries. **PARAGRAPH 1** Hamlet is built upon the basis of extreme revenge and the escalation of the severity of the revenge between characters, which results in a world whose balance has been disturbed. The first signs of distasteful revenge in Hamlet appear early in the play, with Hamlet's disgust at his mother's blatant lust and hasty remarriage. This emerges through evocative natural imagery of an "unweeded garden" and "sallied flesh." These symbols help to paint a bleak image of Hamlet's opinion on the disturbing, incestuous relationship.	1. Note that you don't have to put the thesis as the first sentence. You can play around with the structure of the essay, like putting it at the end of the introduction. But no matter what, you must introduce your overarching thesis statement in the introduction so that the marker is clear on what you are writing about. 2. Although you can't simply replace key words in a prompt with your own preferred topics to discuss, you can add to the prompt by drawing up other key themes, *provided you make them relevant!*

This imbalance[4] came as a result of the murder of Old Hamlet, who reappears as a ghost and also is distressed with the new bleak reality of the Danish court, calling Gertrude, "that incestuous, that adulterate beast." Hence, Shakespeare underscores[5] how Hamlet's intense loyalty to his father and sense of filial obligation fuelled his desire for revenge. Additionally, the ghost acts as a symbol of chaos and corruption, according to the Christian doctrine that was prevalent in Elizabethan society. It also subtly hints at the Great Chain of Being[6], which is a hierarchical structure that God decrees all life, and any disturbance to this hierarchy could have disastrous consequences.[7] This concern was particularly prominent due to the forthcoming transfer of power in the Elizabethan monarchy. In terms of revenge and its position in the world portrait, the character foil of Hamlet and Laertes is important to consider when examining the bleak realities of such a societal imbalance. Hamlet significantly delays his revenge, going to the lengths of using a frame narrative in *The Mousetrap* – a piece of metatheatre which reflects the bleak lives of Shakespeare's characters – to "reveal the conscience of the king." This contemplative behaviour is juxtaposed with the immediate actions of Laertes, who believes "revenge should know no bounds." The two men mirror each other's circumstances in their attempts to rebalance the world, but are ironically met with bleak endings. Ultimately, the imminent imbalance within this fictitious society acts as a literary reflection of imbalances observed in life, particularly in Shakespeare's Elizabethan context.

4. Though this seems like a very simple link, connecting your ideas and analysis in this way (e.g. describing an example of revenge, and then starting your next sentence with 'This desire for revenge can also be seen in...') allows you to seamlessly transition between points very fluently.

5. Don't neglect to use authorial verbs to emphasise your understanding of the text as a deliberately crafted work of the author!

6. This is a great contextual link for demonstrating the imbalance seen in both Elizabethan society, and the fictional society in Hamlet.

7. However, don't just use key words like the Great Chain of Being and assume your assessor will be able to link them to your discussion for you. Instead, include a quick sentence like this to clearly summarise the point of this reference so that *you* can explain its relevance and earn marks!

PARAGRAPH 2

Madness is a controversial conceit throughout *Hamlet* and plays an integral role in demonstrating a disturbed universal balance, especially characterised though Hamlet and Ophelia. It is evident in Act 2 Scene 2 that Polonius and Ophelia come to the conclusion that Hamlet is mad, after his peculiar encounter with Ophelia. However, as presented with dramatic irony, Hamlet's insanity is simply a mask of an "antic disposition" used to combat the harsh realities of his bleak world. In the theatre production of *Hamlet* in May 2016, by 'Sport For Jove,' Eloise Winestock[8] (Ophelia) suggests that Hamlet's madness is fake, which she believes is Shakespeare's way of "juxtaposing" Hamlet's false insanity with Ophelia's genuine insanity. Ophelia, by contrast, simply cannot cope with the imbalanced world that Shakespeare has depicted. Furthermore, Shakespeare validates Ophelia's madness through by her dialogue, with varied verse and prose. In the Elizabethan era, it was representative of the elite class to speak in verse, and representative of the lower, poorer class to speak in prose.[9] Ophelia's madness stems from the devastation of her father's murder, which disturbed the balance of her life and as a result, Ophelia begins handing out flowers that is known to be of significant symbolic value. Ophelia hands Laertes rosemary and pansies, for remembrance and thoughts, to Claudius, fennel and columbine for flattery and foolishness, and to the queen, she gives rue, linked with abortion and adultery. In addition, Ophelia comes to an end by saying, "I'd give you some violets, flowers of faithfulness, but they all dried up when my father died."

8. This is a modern performance of *Hamlet*, which highlights its enduring form.

9. Again, make sure you are adequately explaining ideas and evidence to your marker, rather than making generalisations like 'Ophelia's varied prose and verse represents her madness' and assuming the assessors will fill in the blanks. If anything, it's better to over-explain yourself and ensure the marker can follow your train of thought and give you credit, rather than make too many logical leaps just to write more, or finish sooner.

These flowers symbolise innocence and faithfulness, and more holistically, demonstrate Ophelia's judgement of each character and of the corrupt state of Denmark;[10] for Ophelia, these virtues no longer belong in the lives of Claudius and Gertrude. As such the audience observes the powerful realities of Ophelia's disturbed world. Hence, the volatile nature of human relationships can lead to deception and imbalance in society, as demonstrated by this bleak portrait Shakespeare paints.[11]

10. This is a great example of a clear and concise explanation of symbolism, rather than just a list of symbols or a remark like 'Ophelia's flowers symbolise her innocence.' As aforementioned, don't be afraid to delve into explanations like this!

11. There a clear link back to the question at the end of this paragraph, thus strengthening the overall discussion.

PARAGRAPH 3

Similarly, gender roles and imbalances are also explored throughout *Hamlet* and play a significant role in conveying the bleak reality of Elizabethan interpersonal relationships. A prominent belief of Shakespeare's societal framework was that men were superior to women, as can be seen in Act 1 Scene 2 in Hamlet's soliloquy, denouncing his mother's swift remarriage with the statement, "frailty, thy name is woman," allowing the audience to understand Hamlet's true thoughts about women and his imbalanced[12] relationship with them. Throughout *Hamlet*, Ophelia is especially portrayed as subordinate to both her father and Hamlet. Ophelia is too often seen as the poor victim of Hamlet's cruelty, as is evident when Hamlet tells Ophelia to "get thee to a nunnery." Here, Hamlet is also expressing repressed anger towards his mother, due to their disturbed relationship, as he feels she has been unfaithful and incestuous when she married his uncle and thus created imbalance within their worlds. Ophelia also plays the role of the obedient daughter, though recent feminist critics see Ophelia's lack of an independent will as representative of a repressive double standard inherited in our society.

12. Here, we've interpreted the core of the prompt in a new way to add variety to the discussion, and show the assessor that we are able to approach these ideas in unique ways.

One view in particular, that of Elaine Showalter, is that Ophelia is "indeed representative of women," and that her madness stands "for the oppression of women in society as well as tragedy" (1985). This illustrates the intense inequity in the relationships of men and women, particularly in the Elizabethan era. However, the modern context of this view affects the way *Hamlet* has been interpreted, and therefore paints a picture of a new world with a different context to Shakespeare's.[8]

CONCLUSION

Ultimately, Shakespeare's illustration of the bleak realities in his fictitious world of *Hamlet* continues to be just as pertinent 400 years after it was written. The universal themes of revenge, madness, and gender bring to light the imbalanced way humans interact with each other and the result of relationships that are as tragically flawed as the individuals themselves.

8. These closing sentences directly answer the given question, but also address the ideas regarding its textual integrity to make the essay more cohesive.

Essay Three

QUESTION: Integral to texts that endure the test of time is their representation of what is means to be human. To what extent does this perspective align with your understanding of *Hamlet*?

ESSAY	COMMENTS
INTRODUCTION It is through an exploration of the interactions between Shakespeare's enduring characterisations that responders from a myriad of contextual frameworks can understand his representation of what it is to be human. This is maintained in the distinctive revenge tragedy that distinguishes itself from conventional Shakespearean dramaturgy, *Hamlet*. Through several centuries of reinterpretation and re-evaluation, critics, directors, and responders have constructed observations in regards to misogynistic conduct, the presentation of existentialist and nihilist ideologies, as well as the motives behind Hamlet's inaction and personal paralysis. It is through these critical interpretations of humanity, where the "reality is in the readers mind" (Hazlitt, 1817), that Hamlet remains an enduring construct. **PARAGRAPH 1** The complexity of Hamlet's delay and ineffectuality in his vengeance over the **Machiavellian**[1] Claudius, explicates Shakespeare's effectiveness in "represent[ing] the effects of a great action laid upon a soul unfit for the performance of it" (Von Goethe, 1796). Hamlet is a character foil of Laertes and Fortinbras, as his delay	1. **Niccolò Machiavelli** was an Italian diplomat, philosopher, and poet of the Renaissance Period. His character is similar to Claudius in the way that he deceives other about his virtue, and lies for political gain.

and philosophising is juxtaposed by their immediate actions in the wake of their Father's passing. Laertes is resolute in his belief that "revenge should have no bounds," and so confidently takes action and asserts himself on the basis of his filial obligation. Contrastingly, despite Hamlet's very similar sense of obligation, he instead exhibits the very human behaviours of one plagued by self-doubt, and is reduced to excessive contemplation, and attempting to gather conclusive proof of Claudius' regicide in the literal and metaphorical frame narrative of *The Mousetrap*. It is Hamlet's inaction that has provided a pivotal challenge in the deconstruction of *Hamlet* as a play. Samuel Taylor Coleridge, a **Romanticist**[2] who credited great power to the imaginative faculty, stated, "[an] over balance of the imaginative power is beautifully illustrated in the... superfluous activities of Hamlet's mind," and it is these imaginative faculties of the mind that definitively enhance the human experience in the text. Furthermore, Hamlet's **epiphany**[3] in his soliloquy, "O, from this time forth / My thoughts be bloody or nothing worth," exacerbates his idealistic but unrealised dreams of revenge. This lack of fulfilment of dreams and loss of passion, as identified by the Player King, "Purpose is but the slave to memory, /Of violent birth, but poor validity," epitomises what it means to be human, and highlights its emotional toll upon Hamlet's emotions. Ironically, Hamlet's action of feigning an "antic disposition" led to an unexpected outcome, whereby he becomes truly perplexed by the nature of man – his personification of Yorick's skull expresses this well. Therefore, Shakespeare's accurate representation of complex human emotions has allowed *Hamlet* to stand the test of time[4].

2. **Romanticism**: a philosophical and literary movement from the eighteenth and early nineteenth century that stresses an individual, his imagination and his connection with nature.
3. **Epiphany**: a moment of sudden great realisation.
4. This paragraph is *filled* with some great examples, which ensures that the argument put forth is clear and well supported. The question is also clearly answered throughout the body paragraph.

PARAGRAPH 2

The human relationships developed between male and female characters outlines the misogynistic disposition typical of Elizabethan English society. The patriarchal paternalism littered throughout *Hamlet* acts as an indictment of Shakespeare's Elizabethan context; for instance, Ophelia's archetypal values of chastity and submission is juxtaposed against Hamlet's perception of moral corruption and female subordination. This can be seen in the extended metaphor "frailty, thy name is woman," perpetuated with the repetitive dysphemism "a rat! A rat!" in reference to Gertrude. This depiction of female sexuality is in accordance to the Biblical alternative reading, with women being the root of all corruption. In this vein, Gertrude's actions are symbolic of Eve in devising contracts with the devil to obtain higher societal status. Hamlet, as a stereotypical Elizabethan man, implies his superior nature by his use of an imperative tone in commands like "get thee to a nunnery;" however, through a feminist lens[5], it can be seen that women are helpless due to the overpowering nature of men, epitomised by Ophelia's subservient , "I shall obey, my lord." Finally, although Ophelia's madness is highlighted in her frenzied alternating between prose and verse, she also shows characteristics of sanity, as some of the flowers Ophelia gives away, including rue and wormwood, were used for centuries in abortion potions.[6] This is symbolic of her 'deflowering,' and offers audiences potential alternate interpretations of Ophelia's disposition. Hence, the effective representation of intense interpersonal relationships has allowed audiences through a variety of historical contexts to understand what it means to be human.

5. Referring to a modern political and literary phenomenon helps to demonstrate just how well Shakespeare's *Hamlet* has stood the test of time (and how well you understand the many different ways you can interpret the play!).

6. You may choose to further analyse this as part of a larger motif surrounding Ophelia's naïve characterisation, or dive deeper into the symbolism of the flowers in terms of adultery, death or loyalty (depending on the flower), so you can fit it into different thematic concerns.

PARAGRAPH 3

The presentation of existentialist and **nihilistic**[7] ideologies further aids Shakespeare in highlighting the depths of human anxieties, exacerbated by Hamlet's personal isolation from valuable relationships.[8] Hamlet's soliloquies are carefully constructed, and many of them **foreground** notions of death and mortality; in the first soliloquy, Shakespeare employs a synecdoche, where the "melting", "thaw[ing]" and "resolve" of flesh is metaphoric of physical life and its frailty. The duality on views on suicide between Catholicism and Protestantism is symptomatic in Hamlet, due to Elizabethan England's tensions in regards to the Reformation. This is epitomised by Hamlet's fourth soliloquy, "To be or not to be," which offers a stark contemplative and intellectual contrast, and acts as a **set piece**[10] on life and suicide. The use of collective pronouns in "makes us rather bear those ills we have," reflects the ramifications of suicide to the audience. A more mature understanding of mortality is developed[11] in the graveyard scene, where Yorick's skull is observed as a symbol of "the quintessence of dust." It is here, as well as in the final soliloquy, that Hamlet shifts from the mindset of the "passion... To think, not to act," to his final view of a human's purpose of fulfillment: "What is a man / if his chief good and market of his time / be but to sleep and feed?" In Act 5 Scene 2, when Hamlet finally takes action, he begins to refer to himself in the third person, a bizarre subversion of the play's hitherto exploration of individual identities. This switching of mode of speech indicates that it is only though the abandonment of his self-identity, and thus moral code, that he is able to complete the actions that divine providence, or his dead father, demands of him. Thus, the personal isolation form other individuals can have significant and destructive implications upon the emotional state of any human, which is skillfully represented in Shakespeare's *Hamlet*.

7. **Nihilism**: the belief that nothing in the real world has any real existence; the belief that life is meaningless.
8. This is a particularly strong topic sentence, as it opens with a clear statement about an overarching idea Shakespeare is conveying, then transitions into the first main example that the paragraph intends to discuss.
9. **Foregrounds:** to highlight, or make something obvious by bringing it to the 'foreground' of the text.
10. **Set piece:** a passage of a play that is arranged in an elaborate way to emphasise the topic with maximum effect.
11. This is another good example of *developing* ideas by showing how one example leads into another, thus furthering the authorial message.

CONCLUSION

Overall, individuals across many contextual zeitgeists may appreciate the multiple facets of Shakespeare's *Hamlet*, due to its unified and coherent exploration of what it means to be human. Through the intense human relationships expressed throughout the play, various critics over the past three centuries have formed interpretations of the inaction and personal paralysis, patriarchal misogynistic disposition, and the existentialist ideology that permeates the text.[9] Despite this, *Hamlet* is still able to provide complex representations of humanity and unique ideas, which have perplexed eve the greatest of critics in their responses, further solidifying its place in the literary canon as a highly effective explication of humanity and fallibility.

9. This is a good place to assert your own opinion, especially since the question asks, "To what extent does this align with your understanding?" If this is the question, try to weave your opinion into every paragraph, but refrain from using the words "my" or "I". Instead, you may choose to reference "a contemporary/modern understanding."

Essay Four

QUESTION: How does Shakespeare use imagery to portray challenging ideas about truth and deceit in *Hamlet*?

ESSAY	COMMENTS
INTRODUCTION William Shakespeare's *Hamlet* exposes the unfortunate yet universal eventualities that arise when one attempts to find truth in a world full of deceit. In particular, Shakespeare's intense, motivic imagery of corruption and surveillance cultivates a stark disparity between a world of appearances and the true reality.[1] Though Shakespeare uses a variety of literary devices to portray these challenging ideas of truth and deceit, it is ultimately his imagery, heavily influenced by the Elizabethan era during which Shakespeare lived, that emphasises the societal realities of *Hamlet* and the **vicissitudes**[2] of fact and fiction.	1. This thesis is pretty specific to the given question, so may not be flexible enough to use if you were given a completely different question. Although adaptable ideas and contentions are useful, it's also good to practise crafting these more specific approaches in case you get a prompt that offers a more narrow focal point. 2. **Vicissitudes:** alternating between opposite or contrasting ideas.

PARAGRAPH 1

The corrupt and deceptive nature of Shakespeare's contrived world is representative of the ambiguity of the truth in contemporary societies. In the Elizabethan era, the burgeoning concept of the 'body politic' meant that[3] a monarch's emotional state was **inextricably**[4] tied to the country's wellbeing, as witnessed through disruption in Claudius' emotional state infecting the rest of Denmark. Claudius, through his "incestuous sheets" is the epitomic symbol of the metaphoric "contagion" of corruption. The disease of power has rotted away the court so much that ironically, many of the protagonists deceive each other and commit high treason, as murder only begets murder. Hamlet's search for truth and his obsession with corruption is accentuated by the extended metaphor 'tis an unweeded garden / That grows to seed, things rank and gross in nature" and the imagery of "rot" which dominates his contemplative observations.[5] One disturbing imbalance wrought by corruption imagery is the constant evocation of an Oedipal connection between Hamlet and Gertrude, perhaps indicative of Hamlet's own **penchant**[6] for deception. Hamlet's argument with his mother in Act 3, Scene 4 is pivotal to the exploration of the Oedipus complex, where Hamlet furthers his contrast between his dead father and Claudius, using imagery of the "Hyperion," and the regicidal "satyr" to juxtapose the virtues of the two men: "the counterfeit presentment of two brothers." Hence, it is the understanding of these intense human relationships, through various images of corruption and disease, which provides perplexing perspectives of the truth that are at the core of *Hamlet*.

3. Note that we are explaining this key term, rather than just including and brushing past it. Remember: if an idea or allusion is important enough to mention in your essay, it's important enough to *explain!*
4. **Inextricably:** in a way that is impossible to untangle or separate from something else.
5. This is a clear link from some high-level analysis to the core of the essay question.
6. **Penchant:** tendency, or inclination.

PARAGRAPH 2

Another predominant series of images that portray challenging ideas and epitomises the disparities between truth and deceit are those pertaining to appearances and facades. The entire play is characterised by the hazy distinction between how things appear and how they actually are. This is demonstrated by the metaphorical masks worn by many of the characters, particularly Hamlet. As a result of his mother's betrayal and his filial obligation to his dead father, Hamlet imitates an "antic disposition" to construct the appearance of insanity. His soliloquies allows him to convey his grasp on the truth while still following through with his deceitful plans. Dramatic irony is used to further emphasise Hamlet's deceit and withholding of the truth from the Danish court. However Hamlet's quest to find the truth of his father's death is somewhat futile, and it seems to be something he can never truly be sure of. This originates from Shakespeare's subjective framework, influenced by Sceptical Humanism; a subversion of Renaissance Humanism that focused on the unobtainability of certain abstract truths in life.[7] It is this obscurity of the truth that makes Hamlet believe he is not suitable for this revenge role, "O cursed spite, that ever I was born to set it right." Hence, Shakespeare transforms Hamlet's emotional state into one of contemplation and delay, as manifested through the mise-en-abyme of *The Mousetrap*. Aiming to put a "mirror up to nature," Hamlet wishes to expose "the conscience of the king" by physically manifesting Claudius' duplicitous crimes. Thus, Shakespeare successfully draws a parallel between art, imagery, and reality as he exposes the corrupt truth of Denmark, allowing the subject matter to transcend his personal zeitgeist[8].

7. An effective link to Shakespeare's milieu/social context will add depth to your analysis.
8. This closing sentence directly answers the question while summarising the paragraph's theme, and incorporates a remark about textual integrity.

PARAGRAPH 3

Additionally, the espionage that *Hamlet's* characters engage in form patterns of behaviour that are heightened by the strong visual imagery Shakespeare uses to convey deceit to his audience. From the play's opening line, he establishes an ominous sense of uncertainty and mistrust when Bernardo rhetorically says, "Who's there?" whilst on guard of the castle grounds. This particular scene is set at midnight, with dark imagery foreshadowing the hidden truths and deceit that takes place over five acts. The corruption is also established through the fratricidal actions of Claudius.[9] Based on the Divine Right of Kings of the Elizabethan era, the monarch is all-powerful and knows all, which goes some way to explain why the the "leprous distilment" Claudius poured into Old Hamlet's ear went largely undiscovered, as not only was Old Hamlet believed to have been infallible, but the new King Claudius would also then be seen as someone above reproach. Hence, Shakespeare's use of imagery subtly undermines the certainties underpinning both Elizabethan and Danish society. Moreover, this ear imagery[10] reflects the fact that Claudius' words can also be poisonous as well; his ideas infect the minds of everyone in Denmark. Furthermore, various visual stage cues would convey the imagery of surveillance to the audience – for instance, Polonius deceitfully spying on Hamlet and Gertrude from behind the tapestry provides a metaphorical barrier between the truths that he believes in and the realities that exist though are difficult to find. Therefore, the depth and breadth[11] of Shakespeare's imagery assists him in portraying challenging truths that are difficult to unearth in an untrustworthy world.

9. Here, we are also jumping between several different symbols and examples, but notice how the analysis threads them all together? This smooth progression of ideas is ideal, as it helps assessors see how strong a case you are making for your thesis.

10. Another example of transitioning between different pieces of evidence to make the paragraph cohesive.

11. To neatly tie up the variety of examples we have used in this paragraphs, it's important to broaden the focus of the final few sentences and take the discussion back to the prompt by making more general statements about the thematic ideas, authorial intent, or audience interpretation.

CONCLUSION
Ultimately, the portrayal of universally challenging ideas through imagery facilitates the audience's transcendent understanding of truth and deceit. Shakespeare's *Hamlet* consistently reveals motifs of corruption, madness, and disease as a means to communicate notions of revenge and secrecy. Its articulate form is demonstrated through an Elizabethan perspective, but still allows contemporary responders to form their own opinions due to the dualistic nature of such images.[12] Modern readings evoke empathy for Hamlet, who is critically aware of such ambiguity and deceit in life but is unequipped with the tools to deal with it effectively. This coherent and truthful exposure of life's uncertainties is why *Hamlet* has remained an enduring part of the literary canon.

12. This remark about potential alternate audience views (especially comparing the Elizabethan to modern audiences) is a nice inclusion to end on.

General essay writing tips

Always answer the question that you are given

Going into an assessment with a prepared essay isn't going to get you many marks if you aren't able to mould it to the question that you are given on the day. To do this, you have to attack the question head-on. This means **linking back to the question as much as you can** – not just making cursory references at the end of each paragraph, but actually **integrating key words and concepts throughout your essay.** This is why it's important to have a working knowledge of the text beyond your essay.

Something else to consider is that **you don't have to agree with the question you are given.** You can mostly agree, mostly disagree, or fall somewhere in the middle. Personally, I found that the best way to answer any given question was to agree with it mostly, but provide a paragraph with contrasting views to add complexity to your thesis.

Stand out from the rest

To make your essay stand out, you have to go the extra mile. Get your hands on as many resources as you can so that your research is well-rounded. Find contextual links, unique quotes, things that you agree and disagree with, or explanations that clarify the plot. This will ultimately strengthen your own opinion, giving your essay a clear sense of your own writing voice.

The editing process

When writing essays, it is crucial that you give yourself plenty of time to plan, draft, and perfect your work. It's very easy to skip over things in your essay that you could easily pick up with a quick edit. Utilising teacher feedback gives you another set of eyes and a valid opinion on how you can make improvements to your work. The more you edit your work, the more succinct and powerful your essays can be. This is great for fitting in as much deep analysis as possible, and gives you space to answer the given question as well.